P
CHAR

'There is an intelligence ⸺ ⸺
ish attitude on show in this book that reveals something of a way of being that is fast fading from the collective memory. It is, in many ways, a gift of a book.' *The Oldie*

'*Charley's Woods* is tart, arch and crisp. It recalls a strange, lonely childhood with brisk frivolity and a ruthless perception of other people's oddities, vices and humours... Charley's Woods is rueful rather than boastful. It abounds in lordly and theatrical anecdotes, waspishness and mordant intelligence. ... a tender-hearted, prickly, resilient and life-enhancing memoir.' *The Spectator*

'beautifully wrought, sometimes painful... weaves together joy and woe skilfully, happily.' Christopher Gibbs

'This is a remarkable memoir of an extraordinary life. ... In *Charley's Woods* the author shows himself to be not only a talented writer but one with unusual perception and emotional understanding. For all the hardship he has undergone, he tells his story with wit, sympathy and an admirable lack of self-pity. The worlds revealed – in England, Austria, Morocco, France — are unlike any other and his book will stay with me for a very long time.' Selina Hastings, Biographer

'...deep, amusing, candid, tormented, lively, and insightful...without flinching and with great honesty and such generosity of spirit.' Mitchell Owens, Decorative Arts Editor at *Architectural Digest*

'The sense of the casual cruelties which that generation inflicted on the young so powerfully conveyed. Flawless prose, but a very personal voice passim.' Rupert Christianssen

As a young man

The sense of the earlier books is such that generation inhered in the young as how white they looked. Plenty prose, but every journal work means hairy's instrument

CHARLEY'S WOODS

SEX, SORROW AND A SPIRITUAL QUEST IN SNOWDONIA.

CHARLES DUFF

ZULEIKA
London | MMXVII

First published in 2017
By Zuleika
89G Lexham Gardens, London, W8 6JN

Designed by Megan Sheer
Printed in England

A CIP record for this book
is available from the British Library

ISBN 978-1-9993125-4-1

FOR RACHEL AND OLLY

MY ADOPTIVE FAMILY

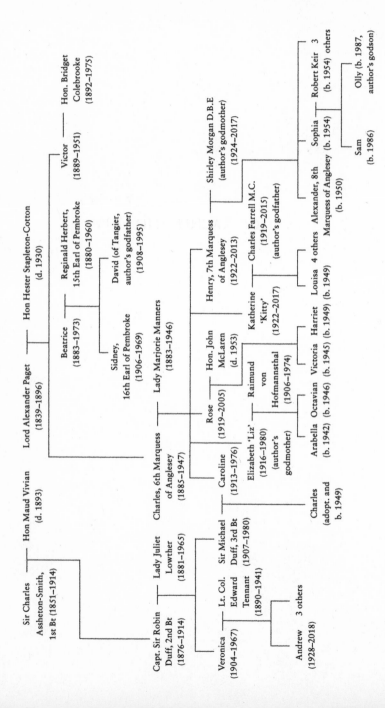

PROLOGUE

THE MINIATURE

My mother's lover, a one-time actress called Audry Carten, had given my father miniatures of my mother and myself by an eminent miniaturist. On receiving them, my father had separated the portraits. The first he put on the mantelpiece of one of the two fireplaces in the drawing room; the other, into the drawer of a desk in the small *toile-de-jouy*-lined morning room. Also in the drawer was a torn piece of paper, on which was written in ballpoint pen, 'Charles David Duff'. The boy in the portrait: me. I was a solitary child in a big house, and solitary children in big houses know where things are. Solitary children in big houses wander, and they learn the contents of drawers and cupboards.

There was another piece of paper with my name on it in the drawer of a small occasional table in the morning room, and yet another in the more ornate desk in the hexagonal white and gold room next door. I was seven years old and I knew quite well to whom the handwriting belonged.

The occasions were rare that I had any contact with this very tall man with a stutter, 'Daddy', who seemed most unlike anyone else's daddy.

Once, when I was tiny, he and I went for a long walk (or a walk which seemed long because it was so awkward) over the sands of Red Wharf Bay. I kept up a babble of infant chatter: firing questions to get answers, and answers indeed there came, bored and increasingly irritated. Once, he and my governess Moussia had come to see me play Mr. Badger in a scene from *Toad of Toad Hall* at Hill House pre-prep school, but by the time I had taken off my badger costume and gone out among the audience, he had left.

The only time I had been alone in a room with him was when I was five or six, ill in bed at Vaynol, our large, white, featureless house in North Wales. My mother was in London, and he had come into my bedroom with a glass of brandy which he suggested I drink: 'Always good for tummies.' I did and it was.

That year too I had been bought an ashtray (as if there weren't enough of those already at Vaynol) to give him as a present for Easter. I was dispatched to hand it to him as he talked to guests in the rose garden in the spring sun. He had looked at me coldly, then turned his back and continued talking, leaving me still holding the ashtray.

Only once did he appear at, or was he invited to, my mother's house, 56 Paultons Square, Chelsea. He came up to my nursery and sat on the piano stool, wearing his overcoat - had he just arrived or was he just leaving? I imitated his stutter, which seemed to me a friendly way to reach out to him, and he went white with anger while Moussia went red with embarrassment.

'Never make fun of Daddy's stammer,' he said.

Somehow I sensed that this was it. A line of no return had been crossed and I would never be forgiven.

Audry Carten (thirteen years older than my mother, not as beautiful but bursting with artistry, with a long face like a foal's, fluffed-up brown hair and pale blue understanding eyes behind thick horn-rimmed spectacles) must have spent a considerable amount of her little money to commission the portraits. As my mother's real partner, she always strove to maintain a good feeling with the nice queer man who had become the other point of the triangle. Michael told everyone that he had had no idea of Audry's existence when he married my mother Caroline in 1949, but this, like much he said, was untrue. All the rest of their world knew. They had been together for fourteen years, since my mother was twenty-one and Audry thirty-four. Audry tried to play her part in the unconventional set-up with tact, hence the present of the portraits.

I took out my picture from the drawer and placed it on the mantelpiece next to my mother's. Within hours it was back in the drawer again.

My father's intention was not clarified until my teenage years, when I read Nancy Mitford's *The Pursuit of Love* and learnt of Uncle Matthew's belief in the consequence of putting names in drawers. But I remember thinking then, with a gut-twist of shock and misery, 'Why does this man wish me dead?'

CHAPTER ONE

A VERY PECULIAR MARRIAGE

In July 1949 the news of the marriage between my parents, Sir Michael Duff and Lady Caroline Paget, was received with some astonishment. Isaiah Berlin, writing in September 1949, described 'the very peculiar marriage of Caroline Paget to Michael Duff'. They were both known to prefer their own gender, although Caroline was the more bisexual of the two. She was also considered one of the most physically attractive upper-class girls of her generation, while Michael, although certainly rich and handsome, was in the words of the aesthete Stephen Tennant 'almost wanting'. The author and mystic of Wilton, Edith Olivier, had observed earlier: 'Of course he's half-mad.'

The news quickly spread, however, that at thirty-six Caroline was pregnant. Most assumed that the father was her uncle-by-marriage, Duff Cooper (no relation of Michael's). This was not a belief shared by her aunt Lady Diana Cooper, who thought that the father was almost certainly Anthony Eden, wartime Foreign Secretary and afterwards the Suez Prime Minister. Caroline and Eden had had an on-off relationship for a decade, and, from a letter he wrote to her, it is clear that Eden believed he was the father.

Caroline seems never to have confided who the father was, not even to her closest sister Liz. Perhaps she didn't know.

Caroline was the eldest of six children born to Charles, sixth Marquess of Anglesey, and his wife Lady Marjorie Manners, eldest daughter of the Duke of Rutland.

Charley Anglesey unexpectedly and fortunately succeeded to his peerage at nineteen, when his transvestite cousin Henry, nicknamed 'Toppy' and known as 'The Dancing Marquess', died rather mysteriously in a hotel room in Monte Carlo after a short life of insane extravagance and amateur theatricals. The estate was bankrupt and the Marquisate in a state of serious disrepute.

Charley was perhaps not the sharpest card in the pack, but he was tall, quite handsome, good-natured, and, in most things, prepared to do what his manly mother Hester, Lady Alexander Paget, told him.

This obedience, however, did not extend to his marriage, of which his mother disapproved. Marjorie was three years older than he was, a grave, sad beauty with real artistic gifts: a pencil-portraitist even finer than her mother, Violet Duchess of Rutland, and a mezzo-soprano who, in the opinion of a well-known singer I spoke to, could easily have sung professionally if her voice had not become fuzzy through smoking.

Charley was also bisexual, and soon after my mother's birth in 1913, he left his family in Tudor gloom at his seat, Beaudesert in Staffordshire, and went off to an easy war in Egypt and Ireland in the romantic company of his batman. This batman became his valet and shot himself two weeks after Charley's death in 1947.

Beaudesert was abandoned in the late twenties (and demolished a decade later) and the family moved to Toppy's preferred residence, the neo-Gothic Plas Newydd on the Isle of Anglesey.

Charley, like so many Pagets before him, was a courtier, in his case Lord Chamberlain to the Queen Consort, Queen Mary. Marjorie, whose artistic ambitions were frustrated and whose original and lively spirit was left unstimulated, succumbed to periods of serious depression at Plas Newydd.

* * *

Michael's grandfather, Charles Duff, who changed his name to Assheton-Smith (after a great-uncle through whom he had inherited his estate) when he was made a baronet in 1911, was a North Welsh slate millionaire. The Dinorwic quarries, the second largest in the world, sent slate to the four corners of the globe from the docks on the Menai Straits at Port Dinorwic. He was a pleasant if unremarkable man, with a passion for the turf, and he had a string of Grand National winners in the early years of the twentieth century.

His son Robin, a soldier, was killed at the Battle of Mons three weeks after the death of his father in 1914. Robin's son Michael was seven years old at the time.

Michael, who uttered not a word until he was six and thereafter spoke with a stutter, hardly remembered his father. Robin had lived separately from his family on the Isle of Wight, with his mistress Daisy, Princess of Pless.

Michael's stammer, which had caused him such misery as a child, was later much improved by speech training with the celebrated Lionel Logue, who performed the same services for King George VI (a story told in the film *The King's Speech*). Thereafter the stammer never controlled him, but was used with great skill to punctuate stories, to hesitate slightly before surprising words, or to point out an observation.

Michael's mother, born Lady Juliet Lowther, loomed large (she was over six feet tall) in my early life, and I was fond of her, but she had been a cold and distant mother to Michael, who loathed her.

Her mother Lady Gladys Herbert was sister to the Earl of Pembroke, and successively Countess of Lonsdale, Lady de Grey, and when her second husband succeeded his father, the Marchioness of Ripon.

Gladys so disliked her first husband, St George Lonsdale, that she always insisted that Juliet's father was a soldier and famous womaniser called Lord Annaly. This was almost certainly untrue, as Juliet looked markedly similar to her Lowther ancestors, and even some Lowthers today.

Gladys was justly celebrated as Lady Lonsdale for being the dedicatee of Oscar Wilde's *A Woman of No Importance* and his friend besides; and as Lady Ripon, for bringing over the Russian Ballet for the Coronation season of 1911, and for remaining Diaghilev's close friend and patron. He paid tribute to her as 'the first person to understand our work in England'.

For nearly twenty years, she virtually ran Covent Garden Opera House, sitting up all night during get-outs, tirelessly fundraising, and deciding who sang. She had re-introduced Nellie Melba as Gounod's Juliette and supported her career, although she personally disliked her. She also championed Vaslav Nijinsky, Anna Pavlova, and Enrico Caruso.

Gladys was responsible for arranging Diaghilev's first London season at Covent Garden, just as Juliet was for arranging his last, at the Royal Opera House in 1929.

With Juliet the worlds of aristocracy, politics, and the arts collided. At her parties at 3 Belgrave Square, these *milieux* mixed, perhaps for the first time. She is mentioned in nearly every memoir of the period. Hilaire Belloc and Maurice Baring were in love with her, and Belloc wrote her a fine poem:

How shall I round the ending of a story,
Now the wind's falling and the harbour nears?
How shall I sign your tiny Book of Glory?
Juliet, my Juliet, after many years.

I'll sign it, One that halted at a vision:
One whom the shaft of beauty struck to flame:
One that so wavered in a strong decision:
One that was born perhaps to fix your name.

One that was pledged, and goes to his replevining;
One that now leaves you with averted face.
A shadow passing through the doors at evening
To his companion and his resting place.

These were considerable achievements for a woman
whom many had considered to be a goose. Gladys is
meant to have said, 'God has seen fit to let me give birth
to an idiot, but I will educate her so well no-one will
know it.' If that were the case, she certainly succeeded,
for Juliet was formidably well read. Some thought she
had no opinions of her own, always quoting those of
the last person she spoke to; but I found her very opinionated indeed, especially about the theatre. She was a
most informed member of the audience and she used
to describe plays to me in vivid letters, which, being a
careless teenage idiot, I destroyed. Others laughed at
her great height and clumsiness - and once, in a nightclub in Berlin in the twenties, a man pinched her bosom,
and when she squealed, apologised profusely, saying he
had supposed she was a Prussian Colonel in drag! But
her want of physical appeal went unnoticed by me.

Michael's anger at the contempt she had shown him
in childhood (she used to laugh at him and call him

'Miss Duff') was understandable. We saw her often, either when she was staying at Vaynol, or when we were with her at Bulbridge in Wilton, but behind her back, Michael spoke of her with exasperation and contempt. 'Here's Granny's hat,' he said to me, handling a stiff puce contraption with a small veil. 'Isn't it ugly?'

I was always embarrassed by my father because I thought he looked so odd: tall, thin, shapeless, with a gormless smile on his handsome face, and, sometimes, foam around his mouth. His contemporaries seemed to think that he looked like a guardsman in an Ouida novel: six foot three and ramrod-straight. His long face was made irregular by a nose twice broken when a boy (in falls from hated horses). His eyes were blue and wistful; his hair straight and brown; his smile compared by his admirers to Gary Cooper's, but his mouth small, lipless and mean. There was also something defenceless about him, which his servants and estate workers sensed. Consequently they banded around him with loyalty. I felt protective of him too – sometimes – as I grew up, but this sentiment was so obviously not returned that my compassion turned inward, festered, and became poison.

* * *

Michael's great passion, even obsession, was the Royal Family. The day he was made Lord Lieutenant, the Queen's representative of his county, was the second proudest of his life; the proudest being the day of the Investiture of the Prince of Wales. Fourteen members of the Royal Family breakfasted at Vaynol before going on to the castle in the county town of Caernarfon.

Michael's godmother was Queen Mary, who often used to summon him to Marlborough House and ask him about the latest London gossip. My father adored his godmother, talking with real affection of her quiet low voice, her directness, and her complete lack of airs and graces. Once he found her reading a surprisingly raunchy French novel.

'Don't you find it shocking, ma'am?'

'No, not at all. It just calls a spade a spade.'

He told of how Queen Mary, on an official duty, was informed that a special lavatory had been constructed for her use. The Queen had no need of it, but thinking it perhaps rude to ignore it, had locked herself in, put her parasol in the bowl, twiddled it around as if she were peeing, and then pulled the chain.

'Oh come on! How on earth do you know?' I asked.

'Because she told me. There was wonderful laughter over incidents like that when you got her alone.'

Another favourite story about 'my old Dutch', as my father called his godmother, was an incident during the war: she was evacuated to Badminton, which belonged to her niece, the Duchess of Beaufort. Her Daimler and that of Queen Wilhelmina of the Netherlands, who was also exiled to Gloucestershire, met in a narrow country lane. Queen Wilhelmina's chauffeur got out and approached Queen Mary's car just as the Queen started rolling down the window.

'I'm afraid you will have to reverse,' said the chauffeur. 'Do you realise that I have the Queen of Holland in my car?'

Queen Mary's chauffeur, a famously rough man, got out and put his hands on his hips.

'And what do you think that I've got in the back of mine?' he asked. 'A sack of shit?'

Often Michael did a comic turn, dressing up as his royal godmother. Once he arrived by Daimler at a friend's house in a toque and a long dress with a parasol, and the charade was kept up as tea was served. Suddenly a panic-stricken butler appeared. The Real Thing had arrived unexpectedly. Michael was hurried upstairs and made to put on some of his host's clothes that were far too small for him. When he came downstairs, looking like a schoolboy who had outgrown his uniform, his godmother looked at him very quizzically.

The last time this bizarre pageant took place was just before Queen Mary's death in 1953. The guests at Vaynol were lined up to await her descent from upstairs, and Duff Cooper - so convincing was the build up - became quite agitated and started shaking.

After her death, Michael never dressed up as the Queen again. So it was an act I never saw.

Prince George, Duke of Kent, was a close friend of Michael's. Once, when staying at Vaynol in the thirties, he asked if it would be all right to take a call from his

father, King George V, that evening. My father naturally listened agog on the extension in his study.

'Please fetch His Royal Highness to the telephone.'

'Is that you, Your Royal Highness? Would you hold?
Clear the line for the King! Clear the line for the King!'

Pause.

'Is that you, my boy? How are you?'

'Very well, thank-you, father. How are you all at
Windsor?'

'Well, your mother's got a bit of a chest.'

She had.

Michael's humour was surreal. He was on his own –
slightly mad – wavelength. If you met him on it, he could
either be very funny, or, like a spoilt child who decides he
doesn't want you in his game, push you away ruthlessly. His only significant foray into creativity was a novel
called *The Power of the Parasol*. The most impressive
aspect of it is the writer's knowledge of furniture; not of
pictures or architecture, but *escritoires*, Jacobean desks,
and Sheraton chairs, described with a dealer's knowledge
of detail. The plot is frankly puerile. His friend Robert
Heber-Percy appears as Robert Oddman, and a Queen
Mary character called Lady Ellerdale jumps from an aeroplane using her parasol as a parachute. It was privately
printed and some rarefied gentlemen have since called it
'Firbankian'. Nancy Mitford was sent a copy, and wrote
to Lord Berners, 'What can one say?'

* * *

My mother's godmother was Queen Alexandra, and my mother remembered bumping her on her enamelled face as the old lady bent down to kiss her.

Caroline was the eldest of five sisters and a brother. They were brought up at Plas Newydd, on the other side of the Menai Straits from Vaynol.

She adored her talented and original but depressed and unstable mother. She 'couldn't stand' her benign, ineffectual father. I suspect she sympathised with her mother's refusal to forgive her husband for deserting her so early in their marriage - and for a man, too.

Caroline was close too to her maternal grandmother, Violet, Duchess of Rutland, known as 'Noona'. She lived in her house in Chapel Street as a young woman. Noona was another gifted artist and a lady of extremes: she loved Caroline, and loathed her sister Liz. One Christmas she gave Caroline a pearl necklace, and Liz a newspaper cutting in a Woolworth's frame, headed 'The Duchess of Rutland Opens Cattle Show.' Perhaps it was because Caroline's looks were expressive and attractive, while Liz, tall and grave, was a true beauty.

My maternal grandmother Marjorie Anglesey's greatest friend was the tiny bird-like Emerald, Lady Cunard. For many years, this famously sharp-witted hostess was the financial backer and lover of the conductor Sir Thomas Beecham. Emerald's box at the opera was always at my grandmother's disposal, and through Emerald, she knew Dame Nellie Melba. Caroline and Liz took Dame Nellie for a walk to the

Menai Straits in a storm, and found her a great sport, who wore funny clothes and laughed a lot. After Church one Sunday, Marjorie asked Dame Nellie which of the children had sung best. 'Elizabeth' said the Dame firmly, which miffed Caroline.

Caroline went to Emerald's luncheons in Grosvenor Square, where she sat next to the likes of Winston Churchill and Somerset Maugham. At weekends she stayed in houses where every guest had a liveried footman standing behind their chair at dinner, and the game was to try and make these footmen laugh. But this was not a world she enjoyed much. Just after she 'came out' and was presented at court, she asked to be removed from the London season to join Liz being 'finished' in Munich. There the girls treated the singers at the Residenz Theatre like rock-stars, hoarding 78s of Heinrich Rehkemper, singing Figaro and Don Giovanni in German. They met Julius Patzak, with a withered arm, whose recording of Florestan's *Gott! Welch' dunkel hier* is surely the best ever (and whom I remember singing the Prologue in *Jedermann* years later). In particular, they adored Frida Leider, vivid but judicious as Isolde and Brunnhilde. They went all a-quiver when in the company of the music director, Hans Knappertsbusch.

Caroline, who must by then have known that she was primarily a lesbian, also fell in love with a fellow student in Munich: a Jewish girl called Caroline Andrea. Thereafter she remained fiercely pro-Jewish.

As a teenager, Caroline had become unofficially engaged to a rather gung-ho action-led young man called Antony Knebworth, heir to the Earl of Lytton. He had been killed flying his plane in a formation at the Hendon Air Show in 1933. Caroline was sad but not grief-stricken. The man-she-loved-tragically-dead excuse came in useful to explain her lack of emotional involvement with men in the future.

On every anniversary of Antony's death, his mother Pamela, Lady Lytton (who, as Pamela Plowden, had been the great love of Winston Churchill's life) summoned Caroline to a memorial service for him at Knebworth, their great house in Hertfordshire. The last time this happened I was taken along as well. I remember the lunch in the dower house, after which I was taken for a walk while the rest of the family attended church.

The Lyttons considered Caroline to be Antony's widow, and Pamela did her best to send my mother on a life-long guilt-trip by telling her repeatedly that, had she married Antony when he had first proposed to her, a few months of happiness might have been granted him before his death.

Caroline also had her own private reason to feel guilty. The last time they had met, on their way to a country house weekend, she and Antony had quarrelled and she had told him she did not wish him to be there. He had been dropped in pouring rain at the nearest station to catch the train back to London.

After Antony's death, the Angleseys were prepared to indulge Caroline's every whim. In her youth Caroline had taken some classes with the legendary ballerina Tamara Karsavina. She was forced to give them up because she got cramp when she went on point, but she had, in the opinion of the great dancer, shown much promise.

Life in the arts still appealed to her. She decided to leave the world she knew, which now she had a distaste for, and train as an actress at the Old Vic School. In 1933 it was run by Murray Macdonald, the assistant to that season's director Tyrone Guthrie. Caroline was a lady-in-waiting to the Macbeths of Charles Laughton and Flora Robson, and a citizen of Padua to the Petruchio and Kate of Maurice Evans and Cathleen Nesbitt. The latter told her later that when she had first caught sight of her in the crowd, she had guessed from her dark curly hair and big brown eyes that she was an East End Jewess.

For the next six years she found modest success as an actress under the name Caroline Bayly, and was, at least in her work, very happy. After weekly rep at the Oxford Playhouse, the impresario Hugh 'Binkie' Beaumont had offered her the understudy to both daughters in Dodie Smith's *Call It A Day* - a day in the life of a typical St. John's Wood family! Binkie doubt-less liked the publicity she brought - 'She Left Mayfair for the Stage!' - but when the actress playing the elder daughter left the cast to have a baby, Caroline took over. Approved by the famously ferocious director Basil Dean, she played the part at the Globe (now the Gielgud) Theatre for a year, followed by a protracted national tour. She also made great friends with the play's stars, Owen Nares and Fay Compton, and with Nares's son Geoffrey, who played her brother. She stayed in the West End for the remainder of the thirties, in such fare as St John Ervine's *People of Our Class*. One wonderful review from the anonymous *Times* critic said that, when she played the Probationer in a Christmas revival of J.M. Barrie's *A Kiss For Cinderella*, '...she moves, she has hands and there are signs that given the right material, she could attack.'

Her movement must have been her greatest strength: completely unselfconscious, fluid and sensual, yet controlled. Her voice, gentle and low but not particularly flexible, was her weakness. Her appearance was both striking and unusual. Her aunt Diana Cooper described her at this time: 'Caroline was a dream of physical beauty, long classic legs, brief modern pants, Garibaldi shirt, her beautiful, sulky, yet smiling face very small in a Zulu shock of hair.' That Zulu shock of hair gave rise to the rumour that the Pagets, somewhere in a colonial past, had black blood. In the company, she obviously tried hard to be one of the gang. But perhaps she didn't try hard enough, as there was always a certain resentment of her social position - and she did not help matters by taking a night off to attend George VI's Coronation Ball!

Her long on-off relationship with the artist Rex Whistler (whose great mural in the dining room is the glory of Plas Newydd) did not, perhaps, show her in the best of lights. But she told me that, just before he was killed in Normandy in 1944, she had decided that she would marry him the next time he came home on leave.

In England, the only two houses where she enjoyed staying were West House, at Aldwick, near Bognor, in the bohemian, intellectual, but patrician orbit of her aunt Diana Cooper; and the Park School, in the grounds of the great house of Wilton, where her gay cousin David Herbert had set up camp. Caroline never much liked the big house at Wilton, where Charley Anglesey's sister Bee, Lady Pembroke and Montgomery (God help you if you forgot the second Earldom) lived in snobbish and disapproving grandeur: 'We never speak ill of a crowned head in this house.'

It was at Bognor that Caroline started an affair with her uncle-by-marriage, Duff Cooper; and it was at the Park School that she met the great influence of her early womanhood, Tallulah Bankhead. Duff Cooper adored her, writing much about her in his diaries. Their affair lasted until his death in 1954. Diana knew and pretended not to mind.

The sex, however, became irksome to Caroline. 'I'm dreading tonight,' she told her brother Henry. 'That little pot belly!'

* * *

Uncle Reggie Pembroke had become fast friends with William Bankhead when the two were young men rampaging around the bars and brothels of the American Deep South. Reggie had been dispatched to the oil fields and cattle ranches, like many young English reprobates.

Later Senator Bankhead, speaker of the House of Representatives, he sent a plaintive telegram to his old friend, by now Earl of Pembroke and Montgomery. It just said, 'Look after my little Tallulah.' This was no mean task.

Tallu was a force of nature. She had stormed theatrical London in 1923, in a play by Gerald du Maurier and Viola Tree called *The Dancers*, a sort of twenties version of *The Bacchae*. It tells of two girls who are destroyed by the craze for dancing, and of their involvement with an English aristocrat, played by du Maurier himself. Tallulah played the American girl Maxine. Another young actress, a du Maurier *protégée* called Audry Carten, played Una, the English girl. It was Audry who stole the notices: it was Tallulah who was the star.

Tallulah was my mother's first female lover and the liaison began at Tallu's house in Prince Albert Road, Regent's Park. Through her, Caroline met Audry, who had retired from the stage after her one triumph. Audry was to remain her partner until Audry's mental illness became too extreme in 1960.

Tallu had warned Caroline that Audry was an inverted snob, and this, I imagine, Caroline found refreshing. Audry was iconoclastic, wild, rebellious, insecure and wonderful fun. Her appearance was, like many actresses then, thrown-together and careless, but stylish and noticeable. She was no beauty, but her face was vivid and her features mobile, her expressions reflecting her good nature and kindness. During my childhood at any rate, she loved me and taught me to be fascinated by theatre history and to revere Shakespeare. It was a marvellous legacy.

It was, I think, a serious mistake for her to abandon her acting career, just when she was about to soar. I caught glimpses of her power as an emotional actress in the sheer individuality and intelligence of her reading of poetry. Her wonderful talent and creative energies had nowhere to go. She tried to channel them into writing plays, for which she had only a modest gift, and painting, for which she had no gift at all. And she suffered.

Caroline's relationship with Audry was secretive. Audry only once came to stay at Plas Newydd, and that was when Charley and Marjorie were away. They had a lesbian circle of friends, interesting and successful women like the comedienne Beatrice Lillie; the double-act Gwen Farrar and Norah Blaney; Noel Streatfeild, the children's author; and her friend Rachel Leigh-White. None of them were ever invited home to North Wales.

* * *

During the war, Caroline and Audry were drivers for the Auxiliary Fire Service, the light rescue teams who were called to deal with the bomb damage during the Blitz. Here they saw some truly horrifying sights - bodies blown apart and people in dreadful distress - which must have had a lasting effect on them both. But they never spoke of it to others. After the Blitz, Caroline worked in a factory, soldering on wires for radios. She loved the working girls whom she sat alongside. They all talked of sex as a fine art, describing it with a delicacy and humour far removed from the upper-class assumption that the lower orders just rutted and slept.

Lesbianism made Caroline's character opaque, mysterious and intriguing. These characteristics suited her dark beauty, sad eyes, and wild dark hair. Clothes were of little importance to her, but when dressed as a woman, her dress was always expensive, though discreet. In the country, or casually in London, she had a weakness for slacks and men's sweaters. There was an incomparable stillness about her. She always listened beautifully - although I'm not sure she often heard much. Her movements were lithe and sexy. She was very much of the present, in the moment.

In 1949 when she became pregnant, she was in no position to get married. She was already married to Audry.

To begin with, she wanted to have the baby and stay single, but her sisters dissuaded her. It was David Herbert, cousin to both Michael and Caroline, who suggested Michael as a husband. It did not take much to persuade him. He wanted his family allied to the Pagets across the water. He liked the idea of marrying a Marquess's daughter and most of all he wanted an heir. He was prepared to be the father of this first child, which was not his, if there were more to follow. More humanly, he had been fond of Caroline ever since he met her as a boy of fourteen. He had been brought over to Plas Newydd to meet the Pagets, who had just moved there from Beaudesert. She was an enchanting child of seven. He was also devoted to Marjorie Anglesey, who had always been kind to him.

Caroline consulted her brother Henry, now Marquess of Anglesey. Should she marry a half-wit? More honourably, she also wondered if such a match would be fair to Michael, given the existence of Audry. But Michael was adamant. He wrote, 'Caroline you must marry me. If you do not you will FALL BY THE WAYSIDE.'

So they were married at the Caxton Hall in July 1949. Her sister Liz gave a small reception at her house at 15 Connaught Square. Cecil Beaton took the photographs. Also present was the tall and gangly Micky Renshaw (Michael's ex-lover and best man), as well as Juliet Duff, Diana and Duff Cooper, Liz's husband Raimund, and their two small children, Arabella and Octavian.

Very deliberately not present at the wedding was Michael's sister, Veronica Tennant, a widow who was then living in a shared alcoholic haze with the distinguished portrait painter Anthony Devas. Veronica had four children, the eldest of whom, Andrew, was Michael's heir, and therefore stood to inherit the Vaynol estate. Veronica had no intention of allowing this immoral woman and her bastard to wreck her son's hopes, thus damaging her own future. She was prepared to take drastic steps.

Veronica had always been protective of her vulnerable younger brother, and had sorted out the mess surrounding a brief first marriage Michael had stupidly made in the thirties. Michael felt loyal to her in his way. He hated parting with money but always ensured that his mother and sister were well provided for: Juliet at Bulbridge, Veronica in a very pretty house in Somerset.

Veronica was quite prepared to have recourse to law to stop Caroline's progeny from disinheriting her son. She demanded that, when the child was born, blood tests should be taken to prove that Michael was not the father.

Meanwhile, in the way of first pregnancies, Caroline had grown huge. She and Audry decided to have a holiday in Ireland, staying with their friend Rachel Leigh-White, who had a cottage on Bantry Bay.

Michael was outraged. 'We've only just got married and already she's gone off with another woman!' he said to my mother's sister, Rose, who had to explain that Caroline had known Audry since she was nineteen. 'Oh, that's all right then!' he had replied.

Audry came to stay at Vaynol before the two departed from Holyhead to Dun Laoghaire. Motoring south to Bantry, they stopped for lunch in Cork at a little town called Dunmanway, about which there will be more to say.

CHAPTER TWO

THE ADOPTED KITTEN

As a small boy of three, I used to have read to me a book specially commissioned by Audry's sister, and illustrated by a North Welsh neighbour. *The Adopted Kitten* was the story of two cats who couldn't have kittens, but found an orphaned one and adopted it: 'We love you more because we chose you.'

There was another book called *Moses in the Bulrushes*: '...and Pharaoh's daughter looked at the baby in the basket and loved him as her own and brought him up as her own.'

The facts were these; or at least the facts given out were these. A few days before Christmas 1949, Caroline was rushed to Guy's Hospital, where she was delivered of a dead baby boy after a labour that nearly killed her. Back at Paultons Square, she was nursed by Audry, Juliet Duff, and a new older friend, Irene Carisbrooke. Irene said to Audry, 'This is the first time I've ever seen Juliet cry.'

But ten days later (and over Christmas too) a baby boy appeared, apparently acquired in the fastest adoption on record.

Drino and Irene, Marquess and Marchioness of Carisbrooke, were a couple of sixty, old friends of

Michael's. Irene - much to Michael's jealousy - was swiftly becoming a close friend of Caroline's. Drino was Queen Victoria's grandson. As Prince Alexander of Battenberg, he had spent his childhood at Osborne and Windsor, where his widowed mother Princess Beatrice, the Queen's youngest daughter, existed as her mother's un-thanked slave.

Drino was a great snob. At the outbreak of the First World War the German princelings living in England had had to give up their titles, and Drino (much to his outrage, as he thought he ought to have been made a Duke) had become Marquess of Carisbrooke. Drino was a small gay man with a dent in the top of his bald head due to trepanning, which fascinated me. Irene, the Earl of Londesborough's daughter and a cousin of Edith, Osbert and Sacheverell Sitwell, was a tall, thin woman with a kind face and eyes that sparkled like diamonds. Drino was not much liked (although he was always lovely to me) but Irene was universally adored, and many looked upon her as a saint.

Irene's great friend was Princess Alice, granddaughter of Queen Victoria, who was married to Queen Mary's brother, the Earl of Athlone, erstwhile Governor-General of Canada. Princess Alice's great cause back in England was the Adoption Association. There was a huge need to find adoptive parents for unwanted children in the baby boom following the Second World War. Princess Alice backed it to the hilt and sought support from the powerful for the director of the society, the redoubtable Mrs. Plummer. Mrs. Plummer personally supervised every single adoption and physically collected and handed over the babies herself.

Michael always told me that he had collected me from Princess Alice at Claridge's Hotel. A likely story and, like much else of what he said, pure fantasy.

But most of my parents' friends, and even some members of my mother's family, including her brother Henry, thought that I was Caroline's illegitimate child by either Duff Cooper or Anthony Eden. They believed that some form of skulduggery had been engineered by Princess Alice and Irene, bargaining with Michael and Veronica to keep the estate in Michael's biological family. I was also, as I was to discover many years later, the only child ever adopted without being given a number, or any traceable adoption papers.

Elizabeth Winn, a dear friend of all of us, told me, 'They said Caroline adopted you but you looked exactly like her.'

Caroline certainly wanted me to look exactly like her. She grew my dark brown curly hair long, so it was just like hers, at a time when it was most odd for a little boy to have long hair.

Years later I realised that nearly everybody who knew me believed that I was Caroline's illegitimate son, and most thought that my father was Anthony Eden. Later other fathers joined the parade: the conductor Malcolm Sargent, the comedian and dancer Walter Crisham (who was, as far as I know, completely gay), and even David Stuart, the agent of the Vaynol estate.

Not until after my parents' deaths was I aware of any of these rumours.

I imagined everyone knew what I had been told by my new mother: that my parents had been killed in a car crash, that my father was a professor and that my mother came from a family of clergymen. *The Adopted Kitten* had been specially written for me because Caroline had disliked the Adoption Association's own publication.

Someone once asked a close friend of my family the truth of my origins, and was told, 'Michael is the most indiscreet man in the world, and Caroline open and honest, but they don't speak about it and it is clear that you can't ask them.'

I believe Caroline wanted to keep everyone in the dark. She liked the mystery. I think it was she who encouraged the belief that I was Malcolm Sargent's son because she thought that it might help my adolescent musical ambitions. I was the understudy for her baby who died. And, because I looked like her when I was a child, I was a most successful one.

I was born on 18th October 1949.

When I arrived at Vaynol with my Nanny for the first time, policemen were - quite by coincidence - stationed on the docks at Port Dinorwic. Thus a rumour started locally, and spread like wildfire throughout North Wales, that I was a Royal baby, no less than the illegitimate son of the nineteen-year-old Princess Margaret and Group Captain Peter Townsend. It was a rumour that would not go away, and it was to return again and again and cause a great deal of fascinated speculation. It still does today.

On Easter Day 1950, I was christened in the small chapel at Vaynol, wearing the Paget christening robes. Irene Carisbrooke and aunts Liz von Hofmannsthal and Shirley Anglesey were my Godmothers; Duff Cooper, David Herbert, and my maternal aunt Kitty's husband Charles Farrell my Godfathers. After Charley Anglesey, I was called Charles. After both David Herbert and the patron saint of Wales, David. Saintly John Jones, the mystic Bishop of Bangor, baptised me.

CHAPTER THREE

THE TOY THEATRE

By the time I knew her, my grandmother Juliet looked like a huge old man. Six foot and one inch tall, aquiline and large-boned, with amused, wistful eyes and an enchanting smile, her blue-tinged hair was tightly permed with a roll all the way round, like a pie-crust. Her great height had been a curse. She had been much mocked and she knew it. Her enormous feet were encased in the flattest of bespoke shoes and she stood with her knees bent. So many writers and artists had sought the *cachet* of knowing her and then laughed at her behind her back. Why she was such a joke was puzzling. Proud of her Russian forebears (one of the Lady Pembrokes had been a Woronzov, who were hereditary governors of the Yalta), she had spent two long periods in St. Petersburg before the revolution. She spoke Russian fluently and Rudolf Nureyev, when he met her, was astonished to hear the accents of the Tsar's court. All her correspondence with Diaghilev was in perfect French, and when I once asked her to translate some quite tricky school German, she rattled through it without pause. Her memory was one of the two most comprehensive I have ever come across, and her reading prodigious.

If the *Oxford Dictionary of Quotations* failed, there was always Granny. When, at fourteen, I played Mr. Puff in Sheridan's *The Critic* at school, Granny knew most of the lines.

Intellectual she was not; a walking storehouse of information she was. She had also seen virtually every noted performance of theatre, ballet and opera of the previous half century, and remembered them all. (Although, curiously - and to my disappointment - not Henry Irving, whose acting her mother Gladys had not admired.)

Her voice was soft and pampered, and she had never had to draw her own bedroom curtains in her life, but for a woman of her generation and class, she was surprisingly un-snobbish. Being amusing, original or just the friend of a friend was enough to make someone worthwhile in her eyes.

The young found her easy too. I remember one young man at Vaynol, who had been dreading the idea of sitting next to her at dinner, finding the experience relaxing and pleasurable.

Bulbridge, her house just outside the walls of Wilton, had a rather frigid elegance, with Aubusson carpets and hard Jacob chairs which were extremely uncomfortable; indeed there was only one small room, off the salon, which had comfortable chairs, and here Granny sat crocheting or writing letters at a small desk. In general the furniture was better suited to the bustles and frock coats of the days when ladies and gentlemen sat up straight rather than comfortably.

For me, the blight of Bulbridge was the butler Andrews, who had for many years lived in a *ménage-à-trois* with Mrs. Andrews and Lily, my grandmother's maid. Andrews disliked me (I think because he knew I was not really Juliet's grandson) and was always unfriendly. Any little humiliation he could inflict upon me clearly gave him pleasure; it delighted him to tell me off for bringing mud into the house, or to send me upstairs to make myself more presentable.

The food at Bulbridge was rich, heavy, and Edwardian. Once, Andrews contemptuously picked up my half-eaten plate of *pâté de foie-gras* (which as a boy of thirteen I found quite disgusting) and put it on the floor for the dog.

Juliet crocheted me two blankets, one blue, one pink. I had the blue one on my bed until I was in my thirties. Also, when I was seven, she gave me a Pollock's toy theatre, which came with two Victorian pantomimes and a complete book of sets and cut-out figures for *Hamlet,* taken from the Olivier film.

This theatre, which I assembled, was a joy to me. I made my mother and Audry (who corrected my misreading - 'O cursed spite' not 'O cursed spirit'!) sit through long performances.

So Juliet was loved by her grandson who wasn't really her grandson. But she was greatly disliked by her two children - my father and Aunt Veronica - both of whom were indisputably hers.

Clearly Michael, shy, stammering, seemingly half-witted, had completely appalled her, and she couldn't bear to have him around. Exactly what humiliations were heaped on Veronica I don't know, but she hated her mother and they hardly spoke (although Juliet was fond of two of Veronica's four children). But when Juliet died, Veronica demonstrated an almost ornate sorrow, sobbing and wailing at the funeral, where I read a lesson, and breaking down dramatically every time someone expressed his or her condolences. There is no grief, as I later discovered myself, like the grief of the guilty.

Shortly after Captain Sir Robin Duff's death in the First World War, Juliet had married a Major Keith Trevor. It became part of family lore that on hearing this news, Belloc had lamented,

I've had enough
of Juliet Duff.
And I will never
love Juliet Trevor.

This marriage did not last long because Juliet, upon walking into the drawing room at Vaynol, found the Major with his hand up the teenage Veronica's skirt.

He tried to bugger Michael in the boathouse too (or so Michael claimed) but there were obviously no hard feelings, as it were, for I remember my father cheerfully introducing me to Major Trevor, by then a rather diffident elderly gentleman, in White's Club.

The reason for the levity of Michael's account of these actions was to show Juliet as the ludicrous figure which he wanted her to be: a buffoon, who discovered her husband seducing her disliked daughter. However, since reading Oliver James's *Not In Your Genes* (2016), I now suspect that Michael was the victim of real sexual abuse by his stepfather, and that this froze him emotionally at the age of thirteen or fourteen.

* * *

For house parties (and for two weeks every summer) Juliet was driven from Wiltshire to North Wales in a mini by her companion, walker, amanuensis, best friend, and enchanter, a man thirty years younger than she was. Tall; a permanently startled and amused look on his much surgically-altered face; an insecure red toupee on his head; a life-enhancer, called Simon Fleet.

To call Simon 'camp' would be to belittle that magician, whose personality had so many drawers and cabinets stuffed full of exotica, beauty and joy. To call his clothes 'theatrical' would be to take the splendour away from what was an outward manifestation of the colour and vividness with which he responded to the world, his disregard for (but not contempt of) restriction, or convention, or anything that was not adventurous and not generous. He and Juliet always arrived in North Wales by mid-afternoon, having stopped on their way to see some strange house, shop or historical site Simon knew about.

Simon had been born Harry Carnes in 1910. As a young man he had written a fan letter to Caroline's grandmother Violet, Duchess of Rutland, and had been asked to call. There he had met Diana Cooper, who had recognized his rarity and got him a job as a walk-on (and as a walker for her) in Max Reinhardt's production of *The Miracle* with Diana herself as the Madonna, which had toured extensively in 1932.

Harry and Michael had met, had a brief affair and written a play together called *Back Your Fancy* in 1938. They had taken it to Tom Arnold, Ivor Novello's friend and impresario, who said, 'I'll put it on even if it stinks!' That was a mistake because obviously it did.

At the Manchester Opera House, where it opened its hopefully pre-London try-out, Juliet designed the costumes and said to Michael, 'Who is that hysterical young man?' It was Harry Carnes, jumping about trying to galvanize the flagging company.

The production was fraught. The celebrated Alice Delysia, playing the lead, said in her heavy French accent to Tom Arnold's mother, 'Your son is not only a crook, he is a boogair!'

The play died in Manchester, but Juliet and Harry's bizarre, symbiotic, yet wonderful friendship was born.

During the war, Harry joined the Merchant Navy and decided to change his name to 'Simon Sailor'.

From this he was dissuaded, so he compromised with 'Simon Fleet'. He also had his *retroussé* nose changed into that of a pug, which all considered a great pity.

Simon moved into Bulbridge, and thinking that rather more was required of him than sympathy, made a pass at Juliet, by saying rather tactlessly, 'Come on, old girl. How about it?'

Juliet was quite horrified. 'Get out of my house at once! Get out!' she shrieked. 'I don't want to go to bed with anything but my book!'

So Simon was turned out in the middle of the night, and went to wake up David Herbert, who had just turned off his light at the Park School. David took him in and promised to mediate in the morning. This he did, and Simon was forgiven, and re-admitted to Juliet's life until her death nearly twenty years later.

In London, Simon lived in a little castellated house in Bury Walk, off the Fulham Road. It was known as 'The Gothic Box' and had been left to him by the great stage designer Sophie Fedorovitch. Here was a cornucopia, crammed with objects of oddity, flair and fun.

Apart from the small allowance he received from my grandmother (who like her son was extremely stingy), Simon made a living as the sale-room correspondent of *The Observer*, and as a pimp for his married gay friends. My father and Sidney Pembroke called him a 'Madame'. A simple dinner was given in the one room downstairs, and then boy and client went to the one room upstairs for a bit of 'trousers off', as he called it. He used to service his favourite clients himself: Harold Nicolson, Raymond Mortimer and Drino Carisbrooke. (For fun, Simon had bought an old headboard with the Hesse and Rhine coronet and arms emblazoned on it. Little Drino, standing up naked on the bed to inspect it, had been outraged: 'How dare you, you're not entitled to it!')

Those of us who knew Simon – men and women – became a club, talking of him and of our gratitude that his gusto, generosity and goodness affected our lives. Simon was so much of the present moment. He woke each morning thinking, 'What has this day got to offer me, and for me to offer others?' But his influence on those who didn't share his essential goodness, and even strength, was not so happy.

After Juliet's death in 1965, his life lost its purpose. He survived for just over a year, dying at fifty-six after falling down the steep stairs of the Gothic Box and having a stroke. Or maybe it was the other way round; we never knew.

His boyfriend, the artist Martin Newell, became one of the most beloved friends of my early manhood.

* * *

Another guest, always in a fluster, always with a story of disaster on the journey - a winter train with no heating, a dining-car discontinued at Crewe, impertinence from fellow passengers - was my father's greatest friend, the photographer and stage-designer Cecil Beaton.

Cecil lived his busy life in a great rush. He had frequently only flown in from America the day before (more stories of crises and catastrophes) and was usually the first to leave, dashing off to assignments at Windsor, in Paris, or in America again. From the way he talked, it seemed he had a glorious life.

Cecil was accorded special treatment by my mother, who adored him: he was allowed to stay in bed all morning while he wrote his diaries and made his plans, as she hovered and fussed over him at the slightest snuffle or twinge. This of course, was just what he wanted. But when he came downstairs shortly before lunch, dandified and cologned, oh boy, how he sang for his supper! Photographing, painting, talking. He never - not for one second - stopped working. Not performing, working. Every moment was constructively used. Growing up surrounded by my parents' indolent families and friends, I had never seen anything like it. I was both dazzled and daunted.

I once helped him compose a letter to Dr. Richard Beeching, the Chairman of British Rail, about the disgraceful train service between Euston and Bangor. Thereafter that was my identity for him:

'Charley!' he would bleat. 'You'll know what to do. You wrote that marvellous letter to that ghastly Dr. Beeching.'

I once, most insolently, told him that I disliked his designs for *Turandot* at Covent Garden.

'Oh Charley,' he wailed, 'I can never talk to you again but weren't they awful! That hideous yellow curtain behind Ping, Pang and Pong. It was meant to be a dim gold glow. They got it all wrong!'

Cecil was a great clown too: contriving to fall into the lake to amuse Princess Marina, or being so incompetent with a camera that one wondered how he ever managed to take a photograph at all. 'Oh God! Which way round do I hold this? I have no idea whether the silly woman has put a film in it or not...'

Today, as an elderly theatre historian, I rate his work for the stage very highly. In my opinion it is superior to that of all the other mid-twentieth century decorative designers, like Oliver Messel or Berkeley Sutcliffe, because of its cleverness, wit, and sheer theatrical verve and cheek. (Only Rex Whistler, who never had time to develop, might have surpassed him). Furthermore, he always longed to break from naturalism into the symbolic, expressionist or surreal. Even his costumes for the film of *My Fair Lady* strain to burst the boundaries of good sense and likelihood, spilling into the strange and overstated. And they are so witty and gorgeous. As Alan Jay Lerner said, they manage to combine elegance and humour at the same time.

As a diarist, he could hardly be more vivid or entertaining, but his truthfulness is a little suspect. In the one published entry in which I play a part - when Cecil took it upon himself to tell us how shameful it would be if Juliet didn't leave Simon all her furniture - he is deliberately inaccurate in virtually every detail, from the location of the encounter (which was in his winter garden at Reddish, not at Bulbridge) to the conversation (which is both fabricated and self-aggrandizing). It has made me rather doubtful of the rest.

* * *

The nannies always had opinions on guests at forthcoming festivities:

'Your great-aunt Lady Diana Cooper is coming for Christmas,' Nanny Rattle told me. 'She's the most beautiful woman in the world. Isn't that so, Nanny Ellis?'

'Yes indeed, Nanny Rattle. She's left her lovely home in Chantilly and returned to live in London. All the family - Lord Norwich in particular - will be pleased.'

I was alone in the long music room which led to the front door. A figure appeared, so grotesque that nothing I had seen at the circus in Rhyl the week before could match it.

She had high-heeled shoes, which looked too big for her, like Minnie Mouse's; no stockings; tight tartan trousers with elastic around her bare soles, which encased skinny bow-legs; dazzling but unfocused blue eyes behind large spectacles; and all topped by an enormous brimmed hat with a feather, like Charles the First's.

'Who are you?' she asked, and her voice was not friendly.

'Charley.'

'Oh. Where is everybody?'

'In the pink hall having tea.'

'Well, let them know I'm here. Go on! I'm your great-aunt Diana.'

'And that,' I thought, as I scurried away with the message, 'is the most beautiful woman in the world?'

Later I would grow, if not to love, certainly to appreciate and value Diana. I fell under her famous spell, but it was slow going. Diana did not like small children (unless perhaps they were her grandchildren) and was not good with them. She also once ate an entire box of chocolates that somebody had given me for Christmas, and this was not a passport to my affections.

I also felt that she had dismissed me from her consciousness as being of little account. This, I later found out was not true: 'I was surprised you were so difficult to educate,' she told me as a teenager. 'You always seemed so clever!'

Diana was egocentric and histrionic, with the aura of a great actress. And I mean a *great* actress. No Evans or Olivier had more off-stage presence and glamour than she did when she was on show. She could walk into the crowded auditorium at Covent Garden and every eye would turn upon her. At parties, her arrival automatically became the event everybody had been waiting for.

She knew her power, but she never thought highly of herself. In fact, she thought her reputation was inflated and her beauty overrated. She feared people meeting her were going to be disappointed. Paradoxically, they only were when she had had too much to drink before the occasion that was making her nervous.

When I was a drama student, I lived in her house in Warwick Avenue during the holidays and observed her at close quarters.

Much of her daytime was spent in bed, where she wrote letters, spoke on the telephone, and received family and friends. On the bed with her was the first of many chihuahuas, all called 'Doggie'. This first Doggie had a permanent erection, and I was sometimes asked to hold him under the cold tap to deflate him.

She always seemed to run out of cigarettes late at night, and would bang on my bedroom door to cadge Players Number Six and chat.

I know she recognized my incipient alcoholism because it was an illness that she had been trying to keep at bay all her adult life, with fluctuating success. It seemed to me that her depressions - 'my melancholy' - were invariably induced by the after-effects of drink.

She was by far the most intelligent member of my family. She had a first-rate, if uneducated, brain, because her real father, Harry Cust, was a great deal brighter than her official father, the Duke of Rutland. (Looking at the Sargent portrait of Cust, someone said, 'Look - there's Diana Cooper with a moustache!')

I was compelled to admire the sheer unique glamour of her glorious past: the greatest beauty of her age, Reinhardt's Madonna in the mime-play *The Miracle*, ambassadress in Paris, and intimate friend of so many of the great. Noël Coward's voice impressed me much more, when I answered the telephone for her, than even Harold Macmillan's. But I liked her for what I can only call her qualities as an actress: her sensitivity, insecurity, pride, modesty, selfishness, showing-off, fun and charm.

Certainly in one part of her character there was the self-confidence that comes from absolute privilege, and her bohemianism and disregard for stuffy convention were part of that too.

CHAPTER FOUR

ALL THE ENGLISH
ARE ARSEHOLES

Our home Vaynol, large and white-stucco, was not a distinguished house to look at. It was featureless other than its green doors and windows. Constructed in the late eighteenth century, it had been built to replace the exquisite house in the Tudor compound of manor, formal garden, gatehouse, farm, and chapel, the latter of which still stood hard by. The gatehouse had been demolished and a yew maze planted, which was fun to run about in. The manor house was lived in by the estate manager and was crumbling to ruin. (It has since been wonderfully restored.)

If the outside of Vaynol was unremarkable, the inside was the height of comfort. Michael had restructured much of the interior when he came of age, with the aid of Syrie Maugham. Clearly they were fond of pastiche ornate plasterwork. Sibyl Colefax was responsible for the comfortable bedrooms, each in the new sybaritic country house custom, with its own bathroom. I remember both these ladies coming to stay, and Syrie in particular, with her mannish hair and brogues with huge tongues, like thirsty dogs.

The downstairs rooms were coloured eau-de-nil, white, gold and pink. There were a few good pictures, a Kneller, a couple of Hoppners, and 'schools of' Velasquez and Van Dyck, as well as Sargents and Laverys and McEvoys from Lady Ripon's house. My father loved furniture, antiques, and what he called *bibelots*. He had bought luxuriously but wisely in the 1930s when he had been very rich.

At a pinch, assuming that some of the guests were couples, Vaynol could manage a house party of thirty with a sleeping staff of eleven. (There were usually nine.)

The view was a complete delight: a man-made lake with three islands and a boathouse, dividing the great expanse of lawn from the deer-park. We had a herd of red deer, and the dreaded white cattle: vicious, inbred Chillinghams, who rushed aggressively towards anyone rash enough to approach them. (Now known as 'Vaynols', these cattle are found all over the country, and it is they who keep the name of the house going.)

In earlier days there had been exotic animals: a giraffe, a bison, and a rhinoceros, who came down to the lake to drink and bathe. These animals did not enjoy the North Welsh weather.

From the house one could see the entire Snowdon range, from the Carneddau, Llywelyn and Dafydd on the left, to Mynydd Mawr (which looks like an elephant asleep) on the right, and Snowdon itself in the middle. Directly opposite the house was a mountain, Elidir, with a sloping, jagged silhouette. Carved into it were the huge terraces of the Dinorwic slate quarries, which had given my family its money and position. There was a blast, a deliberate explosion with dynamite, once a day, and we could hear it from the house.

Vaynol is built on the Arfon, a twelve-mile stretch of plain from the Menai Straits to the mountains. It is the only flat terrain on the North Welsh mainland. It was Michael's grandfather's (slightly unattractive) boast that he could walk from his front door to the peak of Snowdon, ten miles away, across his own land. Snowdon, the highest mountain in England and Wales, was part of the Vaynol estate.

In Welsh, Snowdonia is called Eryri. I adored this landscape: the inner sanctuary around Yr Wyddfa (Snowdon); the Pass of the Arrows, where King Arthur slept, and where Tristram was initiated into the Celtic mysteries; Dinas Emrys hill, where ancient dragons battled for territory; and Beddgelert village, the burial site of Llywelyn the Great's faithful hound. Our private lake near Snowdon, Llyn Dywarchen, had a moving island resting on a bed of peat. The shepherds claimed that sheep would step onto it when it was by the shore, only to find themselves marooned when it drifted away. This island we knew to be famous, mentioned by Giraldus Cambrensis and Michael Drayton. Llyn Dywarchen seemed, and still seems to me, the most enchanted place on the planet. It is happily now open for all to visit.

The park at Vaynol, about a thousand acres, was encircled by a seven-mile wall, built by refugees from the Irish potato famine. This wall was punctuated by four drives with lodges attached. One of these lodges housed a family of at least eight in two small rooms. Some of the children looked very odd, and the rumour was that 'they were far too closely related': supposedly the younger children were the offspring of the eldest daughter and her own father. North Wales was reputably a hotbed of incest, and this was put down to all pubs, cinemas, and even children's playgrounds being shut on Sundays. So the only entertainment was enjoying mothers, sisters or daughters.

As in many poor quarrying or mining communities, Methodism exerted a strong and generally benevolent power. Both the glorious choirs and the non-conformism of the Welsh are products of its influence. Although most of the estate workers went to Methodist Chapel on Sundays, nearly all the staff from the house went with us to the Anglican service in our own small church beyond the kitchen garden.

The estate had its own generator, which gave electricity to the house, farm, and estate cottages. It was very noisy and was permanently manned by two cheerful, voluble men in overalls. All the washing from the house was sent down to a cluster of cottages near the Port Dinorwic lodge, known simply as 'the laundry', where the women washed all day, hanging clothes and linen on lines to dry.

The condition of these estate cottages was shocking: damp and very badly maintained, with rotting windows and no electricity or hot water in many of them. My mother tried to improve conditions with some success, but she was always being blocked by the then-estate manager, Mr. Chadwick, a rude and intransigent man, who was eventually sacked. Why the estate workers, who lived in these conditions, loved my father is still a mystery to me. But most of them did.

When the house was not full of guests, I was able to develop an extraordinarily rich and imaginative inner life, wandering the estate alone.

I think on some level I was depressed. I got up at six o'clock each morning and asked the night watchman (a gentle, quiet man dozing on the sofa in the servants' hall, who clearly would have been no use if faced with trouble) to unlock the courtyard door and let me out.

The Vaynol estate was a great document of history. I explored an Iron Age fort with a Roman camp built on top, where Agricola slept the night before crossing to Mona (Anglesey) and eliminating the Druids at Plas Newydd. There was the beautiful, neglected Tudor compound, and the swish Victorian stable block, where the Assheton-Smiths displayed their Grand National winners' surcoats, saddles, bridles, and stuffed heads. There were no live horses there now; my father hated them.

Once, when I was playing in one of these stables, the door handle fell off and I was locked in, with the glass eyes of 'Cloisters' and 'Jerry M' looking down on me. I was trapped for an hour or so before my mother found me; time enough for me to have my first serious panic attack and develop life-long claustrophobia.

During these early-morning wanderings, I came to know every corner of the estate. I felt it, breathed it, and became one with it. My feelings towards it were poetic and occult, sometimes savage and pagan, and never English.

I had a small hut in a wood by the far end of the lake, on the purlieus of the deer-park. These woods are, to this day, known as 'Charley's Woods' or *Coedwigoedd Charley*.

When I returned to the house for breakfast, it was to a different existence, one that lacked the reality of my solitary wildness.

Ruling over the house was the triumvirate of Mr. Howes, the butler, Nanny Thorpe, the housekeeper, and Mrs. Foster, the cook. Although they were both unmarried and had been friends for forty years, the housekeeper and cook still called each other 'Mrs. Thorpe' and 'Mrs. Foster.'

Sarah Jane Thorpe from Stratford-upon-Avon had been engaged as my father's nanny when he was tiny. It was the greatest blessing of his life. The only security and attention he received in his childhood came from her, and she was the only human being he ever loved. 'She saved my life when I was a child,' he said. She was not, on the surface, a warm or loving woman at all, but rather formal and straight-backed. Her hair was always fastened by a huge tortoise-shell comb - which Cecil Beaton copied for the character of Mrs. Pearce in the film of *My Fair Lady*. She always wore a blue dress with small white dots, and drank barley water from a jug covered by muslin weighed down with coloured beads.

She was a Victorian, not an Edwardian. Charged with taking Michael to his mother in Monte Carlo when he was a boy, the first time either had been abroad, she had said to a surprised porter at the Gare du Nord, 'Now listen! We are British and we are CHANGING TRAINS.'

I believe now that she was both sensitive and perceptive, and that little passed her by. Until her death, both she and Mrs. Foster received a salary of two pounds a week and would not take more. She and my mother got on very well indeed, which made my father violently jealous.

Rose Foster did have warmth and sweetness. Small and compact with cottage-loaf hair, it was her misfortune to be a brilliant country-house cook in a house that - until the arrival of my mother - was entirely uninterested in food. My father loathed mealtimes. He ate his food, without savour, in seconds, and sat drumming his fingers while everyone else finished theirs.

'Oh Mrs. Foster, I wish I could just take pills rather than eat!'

'Oh Sir Michael, you're a one!' was an exchange I once overheard.

Edward Howes was, in the opinion of the grand people who came to stay and who knew about such things, one of the best butlers - if not the best - in Britain. Indian Maharajas told their sons (one was my father's ward) to observe the conduct of a man doing this job perfectly. Certainly he ran Vaynol with an efficient smoothness which, unless you were deliberately looking out for it, was unnoticeable. The silver shone; clothes vanished and reappeared cleaned, pressed and mended; toothpaste was squeezed on to toothbrushes by invisible hands before guests' bedtimes.

Edward, from Reading, had been made my father's valet when they were both twenty-one. Before that, he had worked in the household of the great F. E. Smith, Lord Birkenhead, one of Granny Juliet's few lovers.

Edward and Michael were an odd couple. Edward, always polite, but exasperated by Michael's foibles; Michael, irritated by Edward's hovering, and rude about him behind his back ('he's a pin-head!'), but totally reliant on him. They were two rather stupid men, who annoyed each other, but both were necessary for the other to function. Edward was always about to leave the job, but never did. Paradoxically it was my mother, wary of Edward at first, who came wholly to trust and admire him. And my parents' friends revered him.

I was not so sure. I felt that everything Edward noticed about me was repeated to my father. It was quite correct that he should do so, of course, but I never felt he was on my side. Mrs. Howes, Edward's wife, was a sharp and lively lady, brighter than her husband and much liked.

The children's favourite at Vaynol - and the favourite of the regular guests too - was the tiny head housemaid, Dilys. She simply overflowed with laughter and infectious good humour. Dilys Hughes, her even tinier sister Edna, her stern sister Megan, and her easy-going brother Dick, had all been born on the estate in a damp, cold house of unsurpassing horror, in a dark hollow facing the forbidding wall. And on the estate they stayed and worked all their lives. When Dilys approved of anyone, it was because they were 'a scream'. But Dilys was the biggest scream of all. Whether dressing up in funny clothes with a huge cow mask for Christmas parties, or gossiping with the English housemaid, Dorothy Cadman, on the stairs, her cackling laughter was heard all over the house. Nanny Thorpe would shout, 'Dil-ys! Quiet now!' But her laughter made Vaynol a lighter and more vital place, and she loved it deeply. Later, when the family and estate were falling apart, she wept bitter tears and quickly died of cancer in her bed overlooking the woods and deer park.

I was devoted to Megan's husband Andrew Golding, who worked in the house as a footman, and who chose to look after me as I grew up. Andrew had a drink problem and was occasionally sent away to be dried out, so he understood me and tiptoed around my hangovers as he opened the curtains and woke me in the morning. He was a gentle, loving man, and we understood and sympathised with each other.

Another friend was Anne Goodman, one of the gardeners under the irascible head gardener Mr. Henderson. Anne had buck-teeth, loved opera, wore beautiful ball gowns for staff parties, poisoned the weeds in the flagstone cracks of the terrace, and filled the house with flowers.

Then there was Ray Williams, the dairymaid: tough, independent, and strong, she kept the vast churns in the dairy turning milk from the farm into our cream and butter.

I have saved the best until last.

Eluned Randall, George the chauffeur's widow, died in 2010 at the grand age of ninety-nine, and there went out the greatest light of my early life. If Nanny Thorpe saved my father's sanity when he was a child, George and Mrs. Randall saved mine. I loved them as much as I loved anybody.

They lived in a flat in the part of the stable-block converted to garages. Up the steep wooden stairs I would rush at any time of day, surely interrupting but always made welcome with *bara brith,* that delicious Welsh bread with currants, and forbidden fizzy drinks (George was secretary of the staff club).

Mrs. Randall went shopping in Capel y Graig once a week by bicycle. I would wait for her in the bushes as she came up the drive, to waylay her and be given chocolate. 'Charley bach,' she called me until the end.

George was so kind. As he was on duty until late, he was meant to have a couple of hours off every afternoon. But every afternoon he took me, and whatever cousins were staying, out in the vegetable van, a Bedford with sliding doors, to the beach or mountains. On the way, he was hailed by name by everyone – and I mean *everyone* - whom we passed. And he hailed them back. He was the most famous man in Gwynedd. Rightly so. He was such a clown, driving one day to Dinas Dinlle wearing a baby's bonnet that he had found discarded on the back seat.

He and his wife were the beating heart of Vaynol for me. His younger son Derek, as warm and funny as his parents, became and has remained my friend. He is the first person I speak to by telephone every Christmas Day.

My first nanny, Olive Rattle from Ipswich, used to beat me with a wooden spoon, kept in the bathroom medicine cupboard for the purpose. She was a severe, mannish woman in her late fifties, who had a great sense of her own position in the household. Once, when Dilys ran up to the nursery and asked cheerfully if my cousins and I were ready for our walk, she was firmly snubbed: 'I only take orders from Mr. Howes or from Lady Caroline herself.'

After my mother sacked her, her star ascended and she ended her life as nanny to Princess Alexandra's children. After twenty years' service, she was rewarded with a grace-and-favour flat in Lambeth.

During the 1980s, she was interviewed for a women's magazine about her life as a nanny, and she remembered the names of all her charges except me. I was just 'a little boy' to her.

She was followed by a scattering of governesses, who were all meant to teach me French, and all of whom moved on quickly. Then, when I was six, there arrived a small White Russian Parisienne with attractive pointed features and long hair. She was called Marie Britnev, and she stayed in our lives for the next twenty years.

'Moussia', as she was nicknamed, was far grander than we were. Her family's pre-Revolution home, Britnevsky Dom, I always imagined to be rather like the Voynitskys' in Chekhov's *Uncle Vanya*. Her widowed grandmother was running through the money she had squirreled out of Russia, living in the splendour of Park Crescent, Regent's Park. Her husband had been physician-in-ordinary to the Dowager Tsarina. Meanwhile her daughter, Moussia's aunt, lived in obviously straitened circumstances in a tiny, dingy flat in Earl's Court. This lady, Madame Marie Britneva, was a scholar and a Russian translator of great repute. Her translation of Chekhov's *The Cherry Orchard* with John Gielgud is still one of the best. In a black dress, with hair scraped back into a bun, she was everything a White Russian in London should have been: sudden impulsive hugs, flashes of rage or tears, and much reminiscing.

Also in the dark little flat, lying in bed indolently was a grand young lady, Madame Britneva's daughter, called Maria. 'My dear, I just love your tartan trousers,' were her first words to me. Presently she married a Peer, Peter St. Just, and as Lady St. Just became famous as Tennessee Williams's friend and admirable executrix. She struck terror into managers in the West End and on Broadway, and did a great deal for the posthumous reputation of a man for whom she had always held an unrequited passion. Many actors of my generation seemed to know her, and invitations to Wilbury, her house in Wiltshire, were much sought-after. But I never met her after her Earl's Court days.

Moussia was childlike (and sometimes childish), volatile, vital and always warm and invigorating. Her personality was pure *Cherry Orchard*: half Varya's 'Why is God against us?' and half Anya's 'Welcome new life!' She was also completely without guile, and devoid of all airs and graces.

Her mood-swings and ability to catastrophise were infectious, and I caught them for life. I so wish she had taught me Russian, which I longed to learn, and whose literature and music I have always loved.

Moussia married Tony Tierney, then a footman at Vaynol. They moved to London and worked for my mother until shortly before her death.

* * *

Plas Newydd, my mother's family house, was directly across the Menai Straits on the Anglesey side. The house, long, Gothic and ivy-clad, was visible when we walked down to the tiny harbour on the Vaynol side of the Straits. There and back was an hour's afternoon walk for us children, and we could have shouted conversations with our cousins across the water.

My mother's brother Henry Anglesey and his wife Shirley - the daughter of the novelist and playwright Charles Morgan - had a growing family, of which the two eldest, Henrietta and Alexander, were my age.

The atmosphere at Plas Newydd was in such contrast to Vaynol that I found my visits there vaguely unsettling. It was staid, conventional, musical, and bookish, while home was unconventional, wild, sexualised, and superficial.

Henry seemed loud, exuberant, and unstable; my godmother Shirley was cool, controlled, and controlling. In later life I came to love them both, but in childhood I was not at my ease there.

Shirley had trained by correspondence course as a Montessori teacher. For a whole term, when I was about five, I was taken out of school in London and educated with my cousins and a few assorted local children by Shirley. All of us would sit on the floor of the octagon room at Plas Newydd.

Along the coast, in an enchanting cottage in the great gardens of Bodnant, lived my mother's sister Rose McLaren. She was the widow of Lord Aberconway's younger brother, John.

Rose had the biggest heart and most generosity of my mother's sisters. In London, she worked hard and played hard, running a successful flower business by day, and haunting the Colony Room Club in Soho by night. Rose was the only person who was allowed to visit Vaynol unannounced. Her party of displaced Sohoites was always a surprise. Muriel Belcher, Ian Broad, Dan Farson, John Deakin, and a lorry driver or two would be marched round the grand houses and gardens of North Wales, looking like moles unwillingly forced into the daylight.

Rose had two daughters: Victoria, kind-hearted, warm, and loving, and Harriet, quick and funny. They were also both naughty. Very naughty.

My closest cousin was then, as now, as ever, my mother's youngest sister Kitty Farrell's daughter, Louisa. Although she and I have never been the first in each other's lives, I have loved her for longer, and with more contained depth, than I have loved anybody.

Always good at expressing emotion expansively if it doesn't run too deep, I am just as uptight as most Northern European men when it comes to expressing what is really meaningful. I have also always been better at speaking loving words than doing loving deeds. Louisa is utterly the reverse: cool and undemonstrative on the surface, her loving deeds have sustained my life, and indeed made my life possible.

* * *

It puzzled me, as I looked across the Arfon to the sloping outline of the Dinorwic Quarries, what a small part the mining played in our lives.

I was quite aware, and indeed constantly reminded by my mother, that they were the source of my good fortune; that in the mountains, men using simple hand-held tools cut the many terraces of slate, often in great danger to themselves. The slate was then sent, by rail tracks between narrow gauges, to the docks at Port Dinorwic, from whence it was shipped all over the world. I was also quite aware that we were the lucky beneficiaries of the hard labour of these men. It was plain, too, as we drove through Llanberis, that the men and their families were poor, and that their lives, compared to ours, lacked comfort and colour. I also knew that they were Welsh and that, in their eyes, we were English - although both Michael and Caroline had some Welsh ancestry, as indeed do I.

There seemed to be hierarchies of some kind wherever I went, so I didn't question the providence that had placed me in such a privileged position. But being unsure of my origins, I wondered if I had any right to be there.

I had only been to the quarries once, with large party of the Vaynol household. From the docks, we travelled in the slate carts up the funicular railway, before changing over to the steam train when the gauge became wider. I had a ride on the engine with the driver and fireman, and, like any boy would, I relished and was exhilarated by it.

I begged to go again. My mother wanted me to go. David Stuart, by then the agent for the estate, wanted me to go. But my father was adamant that I should never go near the quarries. I was firmly told that I ought not to have any interest in them.

Matters were not going well in the slate industry. Slate is durable and old slates can be reused. Men were being laid off. Everyone was desperately trying to think up new uses for slate: slate bricks, slate tiles, slate furniture, even jerseys made from slate shavings (I had one and it was surprisingly fluffy).

Welsh Nationalism was on the rise, too. Plaid Cymru was taking seats on local councils. The Welsh language was actively promoted in schools and offices. Signposts were now in Welsh above and English beneath.

The wall of Vaynol - seven miles of it - prison-like, with jagged slates on top, was the perfect canvas for slogans. And slogans were written:

TWLL DYN POB SAES.

('Arseholes to the English' or 'All the English are Arseholes'.)

The relationship between my parents was still in place on a public, social level, but in private it was sullenly hostile. In 1953, Michael asked for a divorce, an idea that was quickly forgotten once he consulted his solicitor and discovered what the alimony and support for me might amount to.

Caroline certainly knew how to make her presence felt. With charm and allure intact, she filled the house with her family and objected if Michael invited even one friend. And to his fury, she doused herself many times a day with her favourite scent, Mitsouko by Guerlain, which stank the house out even when she wasn't there.

Michael resorted to the practice he had maintained throughout his life when awash with resentment: he wrote poison-pen letters, letters which anyone might write to let off steam, but which most are wise enough to tear up.

Unfortunately, Michael always posted them.

'I wouldn't put up with it,' Irene Carisbrooke apparently said to Caroline, on being shown the first few. 'I'd get out if I were you.'

But, for some reason, she didn't.

* * *

'Will I live at Vaynol with my children, one day?' I had asked my mother.

'No, that can't be. Because you are adopted, Daddy will have to leave it to your cousin Andy.'

I don't remember thinking that this was an injustice.

My cousin Andy was Aunt Veronica's eldest son Andrew Tennant, whom I had never met.

Aunt Veronica, I did know. She had come to stay and disgraced herself by getting blind drunk before dinner.

I had met her, as I came downstairs to say goodnight, climbing up the steps very slowly on all fours.

Andy, I knew, was twenty-one years older than me, and as the heir of the house where I lived, became rather a glamorous unknown quantity.

Then one day, as Nanny and I were on our walk towards the Straits, I saw my parents and a third figure walking towards us.

'And this is your cousin, Andy,' said my mother.

The man in a fawn duffle-coat looked at me quite impassively, his face unflickering, his eyes dead. Whatever pleasure I might have found at the encounter was clearly not shared. Those eyes gave out no light at all. They were without any inner spirit. Here was no friend.

CHAPTER FIVE

LONDON:
WAITING FOR TALLULAH

During the war, Caroline and Audry had lived with Audry's brother Kenneth and the Cartens' old nurse, in a cramped flat in Paulton House off the King's Road. With the forty thousand pounds that she inherited on her father's death in 1947, Caroline had taken the lease of 56 Paultons Square next door: a three-storied terraced house, with a small studio at the end of an enclosed garden.

It was here that Caroline and Audry lived until 1975, and where, one evening in the spring of 1957, I sat in my dressing-gown waiting for the arrival of the woman who had brought them together, Caroline's first female lover. Tallulah Bankhead was coming to dinner.

Tallu arrived very loudly.

'This is a very poky little house, darlings!' She asked for bourbon, which was not on offer, so was given an enormous brandy, and focused on me.

'And what are you called, darling?'

'Charley.'

'Why, darling?'

'I was called after my grandfather.'

'I know a little boy who was called after his grand-father.' She did indeed, her sister Eugenia's son Billy, who was also adopted.

'Here, have this,' she said, giving me the most dis-gusting lozenge I have ever tasted in my life. (She must have used them for disguising her breath.) I sat, seem-ingly forever, miserably, with this lozenge stuck in the side of my mouth, until I was able to go to the loo and spit it out.

Then it was time for bed and, after I was tucked up, Tallulah appeared, glass in hand, and sat on the bed and was such fun, and she told me that I must always do what I felt like in life, if I knew it to be true to myself.

Her visit to London that year was not a great success. Now one of the famous women in America, because of her hosting of *The Big Show* on radio, she had come to sing a few songs and tell some anecdotes in cabaret at the Café de Paris, which closed immedi-ately afterwards. 'The Germans bombed it twice but it took me to close it,' she said.

When she left, we three and Kenneth Carten went to the airport to see her off. It was the only time I have seen the inside of a V.I.P. Lounge. Here Audry and I waved a banner we had made with 'Come Back Soon Tallulah!' written on it, and then acted a little play we had rehearsed.

'Oh how sweet, darlings,' said Tallu with a marked lack of sincerity, before turning to talk to Kenneth.

I must have made some impression, however, for every New Year, I received a telegram wishing me happiness, and friends who saw her in New York reported that she always asked after me. She, of all people, was concerned that the weirdness of my upbringing might have an adverse effect on my character!

I saw her only once more. In the summer of 1964 she came to England (which she adored, and where she had had so much success and celebrity as a young woman) for the last time, to make a horror film called *Fanatic* (*Die, Die My Darling!* in America). This was in the hope of emulating the success Bette Davis and Joan Crawford had had with *Whatever Happened to Baby Jane?*

She and Audry had spent an evening alone together at Paultons Square, which had disintegrated into a slanging match, later tearfully made up. So my mother and myself went to the Ritz with them, to act as a kind of buffer.

There were about eight people in her suite when we arrived. Tallu was wonderfully affectionate to me, but soon insulted a youngish American who had written a travel book about London. Audry rose to her feet and shouted, 'How dare you speak to another human being like that? Apologise at once!' Afterwards, matters continued in an increasingly slurry but more tranquil way.

I was in my first term at drama school, in the middle of a class, when the Austrian movement teacher said, 'Oh, by the way, Tallulah Bankhead, a famous

Hollywood bitch has just died.' How silly, I thought, for Tallu was never really Hollywood. And, as for the other thing you called her, I know better.

Another visitor from Audry and Caroline's circle was that genius of surrealist comedy, Beatrice Lillie. Bea had once injured herself crossing the Atlantic on the liner the *United States*, and I had wept when she showed me her bandaged hand. Thereafter it was considered that I had 'compassion', a supposed virtue that was withdrawn from my assets when I became a teenager.

Bea continued to come and see Audry, accompanied by her enormously fat companion John Phillip Huck, after Audry's mind had started to go. Bea had given up the booze by this point, and she would sit rather prim and reserved wearing her fez. 'You don't smile much now Bea, do you?' I said, my famous compassion giving me the freedom of impertinence.

She bared her teeth into a grimace, 'Shit!' she said.

* * *

At the end of the garden at Paultons Square, in the tiny studio, lived an old lady who wore sailor's trousers, smoked a pipe, and looked like an old sea-dog. She was my grandfather's cousin, Polly Cotton. Polly had spent most of her life in the South of France, escaping at the fall of France on a small yacht with an untrained crew. She returned, well into her sixties, to work in a factory.

Polly was adored by all the family: naughty, sympathetic, infinitely curious, and utterly without censure or judgement. She had brokered the marriage of her niece Penelope (who never stopped talking) to John Betjeman, and was the confessional recipient of a host of elderly ladies and gentlemen who filed through our house to get to Polly's studio. Polly's girlfriend was the once-noted mimic and *diseuse*, Elizabeth Pollock, also a great friend of Audry's. Betty wore veils with spangles, long trailing clothes in autumnal colours, and more scarves than a conjurer.

This lesbian circle spent much time in pubs, drinking pints of lager (then a very odd drink for a man, let alone a woman). The Phene Arms, their favourite local, had a garden on the street, and I would stand outside being fed crisps and Coca-Cola through the chicken wire. I thought that pubs and pints of lager were very glamorous and goals to be sought after, obviously only to be reached when I was grown up.

Although I was unaware that I was a little boy surrounded by lesbians, it must have had some effect, for in later life I have never been able to take the idea of lesbian sex very seriously. It has always seemed hilarious, two naked women lying on a bed, doing whatever it is that lesbians do. 'Pity the poor lesbian who cannot whistle at her work,' Tallu had observed.

Audry's best friend was, coincidentally, my mother's aunt-by-marriage, Bridget, Lady Victor Paget. Aunt Bridget had been for a time most unhappily married to wicked Uncle Victor, a cad and a bounder if ever there was one. (There is a photograph of him smoking a cigar while playing tennis, a sure sign.) Aunt Bridget said, 'First he married an actress [the musical comedy star, Olive May], then a lady [herself], then a barmaid [which was true].' He died in a flat near Marble Arch with a tart, 'doing what he liked most'. Bridget's father, Lord Colebrooke, had been a courtier, and Bridget had been brought up at Windsor. She had memories - and some rather camp photographs - of Prince Eddy, the Duke of Clarence, who 'liked drugs and boys'. She also had some wonderful photographs of a laughing Queen Victoria on a picnic.

The great love of Bridget's life was the best biographer of his age, James Pope-Hennessy, but he preferred guardsmen. She told him that he was as beautiful as the dawn and they once had sex, when both were drunk. She had also been the lover of the Duke of Windsor (King Edward VIII), when he was the Prince of Wales: 'I met him on Friday. I slept with him on Saturday. He proposed to me on Sunday, and I haven't seen him since!' (She rather despised Mrs. Simpson for calling the King 'David': 'In my day, we called him 'sir' or 'darling'!')

I asked her, when we were both tipsy, if it were true that the Duke only had one ball, or a microscopic penis, as rumour had it. 'Not at all,' she said. 'Perfectly normal, as I remember.'

Bridget was addicted to face-lifts. 'I can't give you another one, there's nothing left to lift,' said her surgeon. Her sallow skin was stretched so tight she could barely speak. Somehow her ears had become enormous and were far further back than nature had intended. She repeatedly tugged at her few wisps of dyed hair to cover the scars.

She was one of the wittiest women I've ever known, and the most generous. She was a Roman Catholic convert, and there was often a snobbish name-dropping priest to be found at her flat in Cadogan Square. She was also an assiduous prison visitor and visited the roughest women. What they thought of this vision of the plastic surgeon's art, with her grand pinched voice and Molyneux clothes, I cannot imagine. She had a great friend called Lady Crewe, who was not a Roman Catholic. When Lady Crewe died, Bridget said: 'Poor Peggy. So unsuited to her new position.'

She supported many lame ducks and gave absurdly generous presents. She also largely overcame her problem with drink and drugs. Most unfairly, some friends of James Pope-Hennessy have written about her with great contempt.

Away from the lesbians, my favourite people were Irene and Drino, who had a grace-and-favour house on Kew Green, called *King's House*. Here I was given proper sit-down teas with a white tablecloth, and always Battenberg cake. I was allowed to help myself to jam straight from the jar, and then stick the freshly licked spoon back in. And when the public had departed, the little gate at the end of the garden could be opened, and Kew Gardens became our own private garden. Here there would be long early-evening walks before (if I were lucky) I was allowed to stay the night in a bed which seemed to have more mattresses than the one in the Princess and the Pea. Drino once came to say goodnight wearing his tails and orders, although these were only the residues of his time as a Prince!

It was fun having these two existences in London: hanging around lesbians in pubs, yet all the while being treated like a little gentleman, my hair cut at Trumper's, my clothes made by Billings and Edmonds, and tea given by my grandmother at Gunter's. All this took place in a London whose wounds from the German bombs were still raw; where the coalman poured his sacks down the coalhole in the street; where I could hear the cry of the rag-and-bone man as I lay in bed in the morning; where our knives were sharpened by the knife-grinder and our onions bought from the French onion-seller, with his fisherman's jersey and beret. And there were still fogs.

My pre-prep school was Hill House in Knightsbridge. In our russet-coloured shorts, we walked in crocodile through Sloane Square to the athletics track at the Duke of York's barracks to play games.

In the class above me at Hill House was Prince Charles. We went to extra-curricular P.T. classes together in a mews house in Knightsbridge. We were once both sent out of the room for misbehaviour and spent the class laughing and making faces in the changing room. American students have sometimes since liked this inconsequential story. Now, I think that the Prince of Wales is the reincarnation of Solomon.

In my class was a small dark boy called Mark Faber. He asked me to his birthday party at his grandfather's house, which turned out to be 10 Downing Street. His grandfather, the Prime Minister Harold Macmillan, arrived after some business and was jolly with us and took the others and me to see the Cabinet Room.

* * *

Caroline was at a disadvantage, for she had to be both a mother and a father. She was a good mother: affectionate, tactile, encouraging; often tickling, laughing and rolling about on furniture and floors, great fun. But she was a bad father: controlling, harsh, intractable and overly punitive. She had, on her own admission, been slow to love me, and I had been slow to respond. But when she gave love, she gave it full-force, and was absurdly over-protective. She ordered me never to sleep with a pillow, so my back would be strong (unsuccessful). She prescribed a spoon of milk of magnesia after every meal to give me strong digestion (that one worked and I am grateful) and only gave me brown bread and brown sugar (in advance of her time perhaps, but everyone else was allowed white and I was resentful). Most absurdly of all, I was not allowed to walk in the street until I was four because she believed my legs would be stronger if I were kept in a pram. 'Isn't he old enough to walk by now?' a stranger asked Nanny Rattle in disbelief.

I was shy and found it hard to make friends with children who were not my cousins. But in Kensington Gardens one day I met the most beautiful brother and sister I had ever seen. They were quiet, dignified and gentle. I had never felt so at ease with anyone of my own age before. Although their nanny was English, their father was a diplomat from an African country. And they were black. They asked me back to tea one day, and I longed to go, but Nanny said no, we couldn't, which was untrue. On the way back home she told me that it would be difficult going to their house, as I would then, out of politeness, have to ask them back to mine, 'and that would not be possible.' At home, I excitedly told my mother of my new friends, while Nanny quickly apologised for allowing me to speak to blacks. 'But of course you should go to tea with them and ask them here,' said my mother. But, although they asked again and again, Nanny made excuses, and we sadly parted every day, as they walked down Queen's Gate Terrace, and we down Gloucester Road. Furthermore, I think they knew the reason.

CHAPTER SIX

VAYNOL:
ELEPHANTS AND ROYALS

'I can't cope with you anymore,' said my mother in exasperation. 'I'm going to ask Daddy to beat you.' I looked at her in complete disbelief for a second and then burst out laughing. The idea of Daddy beating anyone was too ludicrous.

During my father's lifetime, I never claimed to be his son, for the very good reason that I assumed people considered him incapable of fathering a child.

Living with my father was like living with another child, and a spiteful one too; I was competition.

Once I found a discarded model of a Dinorwic quarry railway engine. One of the estate workers cleaned and painted it for me, and I kept it in my playroom. Then one day it had gone. Its presence had been reported to my father, so he took it and put it in his bathroom. Anything else that I found at the back of cupboards and enjoyed (and there was quite a lot) had to be surrendered to Edward Howes, who took it to my father, who usually just threw it away. He did not wish for me to lay claim to anything in the house.

Such behaviour hardly counted as abuse, but it was mean-spirited.

We spent one Christmas in London when I was about thirteen, and had lunch at my aunt Kitty Farrell's house. My father now had his own flat in Cadogan Gardens at the other end of the King's Road to my mother's house, and from there we collected him on Christmas morning.

'Isn't it *awful*, Charley,' he said cheerfully as he got into the car, laden with presents. 'I haven't got you *anything*!' And he looked around at me triumphantly.

His attitude towards having an immediate family was whimsical. His were the unpredictable desires of the thwarted child. He complained that my mother spent too much time away from Vaynol; yet whenever the two of them were alone there together, he was obviously so bored by her presence and irritated by her habits, in particular her scent, that she felt uncomfortable and unwelcome. Although to me they always seemed quite relaxed with each other when we were together.

'He never appreciates me,' she said. He didn't. He saw himself as a victim. It was always others who were at fault. And no friend was allowed to be close for too long, in case they took advantage.

It was the same with his attitude towards me. Occasionally, such as when there was a televised Remembrance Day service from Bangor Cathedral and he was in his Lord Lieutenant's uniform, he was pleased to be seen with a son. But any irksome paternal responsibilities, like spending time alone with me or giving guidance, were shirked. When I was well into my twenties, I found out, from my mother's last lover, that even when I was very young indeed he had begun to speak ill of me behind my back. Even though our relationship was by then in tatters, I was appalled.

But it was useful, of course, to have a wife to play hostess and a child to suggest a family man when Royalty stayed.

Royalty was one of his two obsessions, the other being elephants. The house was peppered with gold, silver, brass, ivory, china, and wooden 'jumbos', as he called them.

His obsession with the Royal family was forever unabated and some of his affection was mildly reciprocated. (Royalty, as James Pope-Hennessy observed, split the world into two classes: themselves and servants of varying degrees.)

Michael certainly blossomed in the presence of royalty. He played the fool; obviously knew more about their family and its scandals than they did; and plainly worshipped them all. So no wonder they came to stay at Vaynol when duty called them to North Wales.

The Royalty we saw most, and whom I liked by far the best, was Princess Marina, Duchess of Kent, once Princess Marina of Greece, widow of that Prince George on whose conversation with the King my father had eavesdropped. Unlike the others, she was a genuine family friend. Still elegant and most beautiful, not very bright but warm, unassuming and easy, she connected with children with a generosity quite alien to her more self-centred sister-in-law, the Queen Mother. My cousin Louisa Farrell and I vied to have her in our team for The Game (our version of charades), where she clowned with the rest. She always seemed to leave her packet of cigarettes (Kent's - was she given them for free?) somewhere and I would be sent to find and fetch them. Once she came with her daughter Princess Alexandra, whose sunglasses fell off and broke as she was teaching me to bow.

Prince Philip, Duke of Edinburgh, whom Michael had known since the Duke's youth, seemed a cheerful and straightforward sort of chap. With the jacket of his suit removed, he played cricket with me on the lawn at Vaynol, and nearly succeeded in making me like it. Years later, I told him I had been a complete failure at cricket and he said, 'So you never made the first eleven then!'

I was not so sure, however, about the Queen Mother, whom my father revered above all. She was called 'The Beamer' or 'The Cake', because years before at a wedding, when told that the couple were about to cut the cake, she had thrown up her hands and cried ecstatically, 'CAKE!' She had two faces, I noted: an upper face with hard calculating little eyes which missed nothing, and observed the world with a marked lack of charity; and a lower face, all smiles and compliments. I was once thrown into her car after some engagement, and travelled with her and a lady-in-waiting for the hour's drive back to Vaynol. She seemed most put out by my presence. The few sideways glances I received were free of warmth.

Princess Alice, that granddaughter of Queen Victoria's who, with Irene, had been instrumental in my adoption, sometimes came with her husband Lord Athlone. This merry, laughing old lady had omitted to tell my parents that her husband had not just become forgetful, but had lapsed into complete silence, except at intervals when he would suddenly shout out, 'Gobble! Gobble!' At that point, Princess Alice grabbed his arm and hurried him out of the room. They returned serenely five minutes later. It was his code word for needing a pee.

* * *

'Is it true that you were kicked out of Spain?' I asked another of Queen Victoria's granddaughters, Queen Victoria Eugenie. It was the one thing I had been told not to say during that August bank holiday at Vaynol.

'No, it is not true,' she answered, reasonably enough. 'I went of my own accord.'

Queen Ena was Drino Carisbrooke's sister and a close friend of her sister-in-law, Irene. Later, Irene sat on the end of my bed and gently told me that I should not have said that, because Queen Ena was a sweet and kind person and I had hurt her. Many people had said this about her and it upset her. Then she told me how she and the Queen had left Madrid, travelling north across the border into France, King Alfonso and Drino having done a bunk earlier.

'At each station we stopped at, just ahead of the communist troops, the *alguazil* and citizens begged us to stay and not to abandon them. Some even knelt. The peasants in the fields knelt. She left because she thought it best for her husband's country.'

(Royalty always see the populace rather like this, I have observed. An opera chorus of adoring subjects, whose blind loyalty is only subverted by a few wicked and envious agitators. They think like that still, except it is now the press and not the anarchists who are the villains.)

Queen Ena was a large woman, who reclined gingerly on the fragile *chaise longue* placed at the end of her bed, as guests were brought in to her to make their obeisance and say goodnight. I bowed like Winnie the Pooh, one hand over my tummy, the other in the small of my back, which she thought charming. Her lady-in-waiting was an elongated Spanish lady of high rank, an El Greco, dressed from head to foot in black. I once caught this lady early in the morning in her nightclothes, which were voluminous and trailing, with her hair in curling papers.

Drino had been staying with his sister in Madrid when he had been arrested for cottaging (importuning in a public convenience). Instead of paying the fine and keeping mum, he had pulled rank, said he was the Queen's brother, and demanded immediate release. The embarrassed chief-of-police had asked Queen Ena to verify his statement. She had no idea what offence he was meant to have committed and said, 'Please don't worry. It is only His Majesty and I - and of course, the children - who should not be seen visiting public lavatories. My brother *El Marqués* may use them whenever he wishes.'

* * *

We had some neighbours who lived at Bont Newydd in a house called *Dinas*, a few miles to the other side of Caernarfon. They were called Armstrong-Jones. Ronnie was a rubicund silk who, on meeting new people, took one's hand in both of his and gazed with practised sincerity. His pretty young wife was mocked by some (although certainly not by my parents) for having once been an air-hostess.

Ronnie's mother, Lady Armstrong-Jones, the wife of a surgeon, had been one of my father's favourite local characters. 'Blodwyn, Blodwyn!' she was heard exhorting a chambermaid. 'How many *more* times must I tell you never to clean Sir Robert's tooth glass out with the chamber-cloth!' She also used to introduce her very plain daughter as 'my beautiful daughter Gwynneth'.

Ronnie's first wife, Anne, had been the sister of the eminent designer and decorator Oliver Messel, and they had had a son, Antony, who was my father's godson.

Tony's brilliance and fame as a photographer had not really registered with my father. Nor, apparently, had it with Aunt Bea at Wilton. When Tony went to take some photographs, she made him eat in the servants' hall. She was most discomforted when a week later he became engaged to Princess Margaret.

I was at prep school when this momentous event happened. As no-one in the press knew much (or at least not much that could be printed) about Antony Armstrong-Jones, Michael, as his godfather, became an oracle of information. However, he purported to be displeased that Tony had chosen as his title the mountain that my father owned, without asking his permission.

Of course, Princess Margaret and Tony usually stayed with Tony's father at Dinas, but once, when I was fifteen, Princess Margaret needed the Royal helicopter to take her to and from engagements, and Vaynol had a large lawn, so they stayed with us.

Just after their arrival, I was given a joyride in the red helicopter. I thought this so extremely kind of the pilot that I asked him to tea. As we walked into the pink hall, the group sitting around the tea table looked up, and I thought I saw a quickly controlled look of surprise pass across the Princess's face.

All the focus was now on the pilot who, bombarded with questions, revealed that the helicopter cost three hundred pounds of taxpayers' money a day to run. My mother, who had already decided that Princess

Margaret was not her sort, said incredulously, 'It costs three hundred pounds? A day! Three hundred pounds!'

Worse was to follow. My mother disliked staying up late; Princess Margaret did not like going to bed early. The carpet in the pink hall was rolled back and there was dancing. Midnight and one o'clock came; more dancing. Three o'clock and the Princess showed no signs of flagging. Of course, nobody goes to bed before royalty. At last my mother strode across to the Princess and said, 'Ma'am, I'm sorry; I'm off to bed now. Do excuse me.' Princess Margaret looked at her with withering *hauteur*, and then turned her back.

My father's young boyfriend Edward Mace, then writing *Pendennis*, the gossip-column of *The Observer*, was staying. He and Tony, who was then employed by *The Sunday Times*, had a reasonably good-natured argument about the merits of their respective papers. Princess Margaret weighed in rather too enthusiastically on her husband's side, and my mother a bit too aggressively on Edward's. A drink got kicked over and, quite uncharacteristically, I disappeared to fetch bucket and mop, both of which were unnecessary.

The visit ended well, however, as my mother and I took Princess Margaret and Tony to see a deserted house on the Straits, which they were thinking of renting. There was overgrowth and broken glass and dead blackbirds that had flown down chimneys. Tony wriggled through a small scullery window to unlock a door, and there was laughter, ease, and many photographs taken by the Princess.

I had always liked her; in fact I had been in thrall to her ever since she had winked at me across the table of an enormous, boring lunch party years earlier. She was enchantingly pretty and her glamour was that of a *prima ballerina*.

Later I observed her, usually after a few drinks, being haughty and rude, but to me she showed charm alone. I found her intelligent, interesting and engaged. Sitting next to her at a dinner in London, I remember our talk, which began with John Osborne, whose *Inadmissible Evidence* she dissected with a depth and precision an academic would envy. She ranged through misfortunes at performances she had attended (Wotan falling off a platform with a loud clatter at the end of *Die Walküre*) and ending with the Crazy Gang, which we both loved. ('Do you actually *know* Bud Flanagan?' she asked, wide-eyed.) She observed, 'Their humour's very Jewish, isn't it? Which of course I love, as I'm a Yid.' (Can she actually have said that? I have always sworn she did, although some have disbelieved me. Her great-great grandfather, the illegitimate Prince Consort, was reputedly half-Jewish.)

The last time I saw her, not long before she died, she remembered me, and that weekend at Vaynol. And more. I liked her a lot for that.

* * *

The glamour of all this activity at Vaynol sucked me in and I felt part of it. Indeed it empowered me. Vaynol was my possession, and my father was an interloper. We avoided each other when in company, and I hoped never to meet him accidentally in the corridors. I did not view the house as his, but as my mother's and mine.

To teach me to think of another living creature, I had been given a small border terrier called Simon, who was unhappy at being owned by a little boy. He became neurotic and finally feral. Sometimes he ran away for hours and returned with a blood-flecked mouth. My father loathed him.

At the same time, my father acquired a large, sleek, black boxer. After the Belloc Cautionary Tale, he was called Ponto.

Ponto was vile. Gardeners were terrified of approaching the house when he was prowling. He cowered in corners, snarling and foaming, and his bark was a bark of rage.

One afternoon, I heard a commotion so explosive from the nearby drawing room that I knew with sudden terror that something truly awful was happening.

Ponto and Simon were fighting. And fighting to the death. No illegal dogfight behind closed doors could have been more vicious.

The drawing room was crowded with guests, who had backed against the wall, terrified. They couldn't get out because the dogs were fighting near the door. Blood was flying.

My mother was squirting the dogs with the contents of a soda siphon, and my father was standing by with open-mouthed horror. Simon had latched on to Ponto's neck and was worrying his throat with his teeth. White-faced and shaking, I appeared just in time to see the boxer fall on his back, and the border terrier start to tear his throat out.

I was far too scared to be brave, but for some mad reason I stepped forward, grabbed Simon by his scruff and ran out of the room. He spat and coughed blood at me, and his eyes were filled with a mad ecstasy, but I calmed him. He was my dog after all.

Ponto, however, was in a dreadful state. He had been horribly injured.

I didn't see what happened next because I was sent upstairs with Simon. A vet was summoned to attend to Ponto, who recovered, but was given away. We never saw him again and all at Vaynol were relieved.

Simon was given away as well, to Polly Cotton's Irish maid, Kathleen. Shortly after, he ran into the traffic of Hyde Park Corner and was run over.

After that, there was a shift in my relationship with my father. From one of childish competition and meanness, it changed into something far darker. Vindictiveness replaced spite, slander replaced mild unpleasantness, and hatred replaced coldness.

The fight between our dogs was an outward manifestation of the suppressed fight between ourselves. I was the smaller, but - for that round, anyway - I had won.

CHAPTER SEVEN

LONDON: PETER PAN NEEDS AN INJECTION

The Scala Theatre near Tottenham Court Road, where every year there was a revival of J.M. Barrie's *Peter Pan*, was the most wonderful and magical building in the world, for it was my first theatre. When, in December 1957, I walked into the auditorium with its side boxes and huge pillars (much space wasted, no doubt) I knew I had come to somewhere I belonged, and it was the first time I had ever felt that.

James Barrie was a great figure in our family mythology. At Vaynol, visiting as a close friend of Juliet's, my father remembered him flicking postage stamps onto the ceiling. He went fishing in Llyn Dywarchen, whose moving island reputedly gave him the idea for the island in *Mary Rose*. Audry, as a member of Gerald du Maurier's company, had played in a revival of *Dear Brutus* (Dearth being one of Sir Gerald's best roles). When the author met the cast, Audry had kissed his hand, and Barrie, to everyone's astonishment, had risen on tiptoe and kissed her on the mouth.

The production of *Peter Pan*, although redesigned, was basically Dion Boucicault's original one from

1904: the Frozen River with tropical beach glimpsed in the distance; the Mermaid's lagoon with visible stage-hands shaking blue cloths like waves; the House-under-the-ground with its split levels; and that magical incredible flying, far superior to any stage flying of today, which is so encumbered by silly safety regulations. There was only one wire on the harness, and that wire nearly invisible, and the entire company flew at curtain call, including Nana and Mr. Darling. And there was John Crook's glorious incidental music. The whole Peter Pan experience (at least the old one, with Peter as Principal Boy) fell apart when Robert Helpmann directed a new production in the early 1970s. He idiotically jettisoned this music, although Barrie had been categorical that Crook's music was as intrinsic to the play as Tenniel's drawings were to *Alice in Wonderland*. (And now this essential music is unknown, for in the film *Neverland*, Nana cavorted about at the start of the play, a so-called reconstruction of the original production, in complete silence!) Mary Casson, the mother of my friend Diana Devlin, played Wendy for six seasons from 1928. She told me the Musical Director used to shake his head and say, 'Poor Johnny Crook, he died in poverty!'

Peter was played either by young starlets or established actresses. The latter, like Margaret Lockwood, were preferable. Even now I can never accept a boy Peter, for I know Peter to be a middle-aged lady with a perm, lots of make-up, and bosoms.

For my second year of the play, Peter was played by an old friend of my mother's, Sarah Churchill, Sir Winston's daughter.

After the Saturday matinee we went backstage, where cast and crew were using the hour's break that separated shows to set up for the evening. A message came that Miss Churchill was not ready to see us, and an assistant stage manager was detailed to show us the stage, where the nursery was being created. We passed Captain Hook's huge sledge, and two of the Lost Boys, already in their furs for their first entrance, stood back to let us pass. (I longed to be one of them.) Flats were hoisted into place; there was a smell of size; and I knew with absolute certainty that backstage was for me.

Sarah, when she eventually received us, was wearing an old dressing gown and sipping a colourless liquid from a glass, attended by a Polish lady in a hat. She looked and sounded like any friend of my mother's, and rather a grumpy one.

'I hardly got through the show this afternoon. I needed an injection to get me through, didn't I, Ivanka? I shall need another one for tonight, so you can't stay long.' She seemed the opposite of youth, joy, and a little bird flown out of its nest. Yet her Peter was the best I have seen: fey, strange, a bit creepy but enchanting. He was a boy with whom you would fly to the outside of the cosmos. Only Mark Rylance, years later, came near to her, but he was the wrong gender.

Much later, in pubs, I came to know Sarah quite well. (She was still attended by the same Polish lady.) She was a gentle, sweet woman, so gifted as poet and actress, but her life was derailed by drink. 'Like many members of the upper class,' her sister-in-law June said to me, quoting Belloc, 'She liked the sound of broken glass.'

* * *

Next door to us, still living in the flat in Paulton House where Caroline and Audry had spent the War, was Audry's brother Kenneth Carten. He was by now a top theatrical agent with Laurence Olivier and Noël Coward on his books, and his partner was the director and impresario Murray Macdonald.

My mother disliked Kenneth, whom she considered a spoilt brat, but, although Murray later told me he was insanely jealous of me for taking his sister's attention away, Kenneth was always kind, and later helpful.

Murray got out of the flat every Thursday evening, when a guardsman came round to give Kenneth a good seeing-to. In return, Murray was allowed to be the confidant of his own little bevy of old actresses: Isabel Jeans (the best Lady Bracknell ever, far better than Dame Edith Evans), Dorothy Dickson (Ivor Novello's leading lady, so pretty and *soignée*, who pretended she was thirty-three and looked blank if anyone remembered a past performance), and a monstrous old bag called Ivy St Helier (Alice in Olivier's film of *Henry V*, and the *diseuse* who first sang that song about only having a talent to amuse in Coward's *Bitter Sweet*). Ivy, who suffered from horrible cataracts, caused Murray endless dramas, and he always threatened to send her round for us to deal with if we displeased him. But she was interested in me and remembered what I told her, which was enough for my affection. I used to go round and help set up the makeshift dining-room table when this coven gathered. Murray and Kenneth were great theatre gossips (and at a high level, too) and there was little I didn't know about who got up to what with whom. It made me precocious in quite the wrong way and, to some of my schoolfellows, unbearable.

Murray could provide tickets for West End plays, at least the kind of plays in which he had an interest: light comedies, thrillers, and vehicles for stars. The plays of Hugh and Margaret Williams I thought, and still think, a joy. A fierce Scotswoman called Lesley Storm, author of *Black Chiffon*, a drama about shop-lifting, and a really excellent comedy called *Roar Like A Dove*, asked me to attend dress rehearsals and then read me lectures about how, if I wished to be in the theatre, I would need to work harder at maths. Her reasoning made no sense to me.

There was great theatre, too, to be found in Murray's presentations. In 1966, Dame Sybil Thorndike and Athene Seyler played in *Arsenic and Old Lace* ('Lace Knickers and Old Arse' to the rest of the cast). And I remember Dame Sybil, clinging on to the altar rails, trying not to levitate, in *Teresa of Avila*.

Then there was Stratford. I already knew I loved Shakespeare's plays, because Audry would direct me in scenes from them. And there was an excellent schools' *Macbeth* on our new television, with William Devlin and Mary Morris.

My mother, Audry, and I decamped to Stratford each July and stayed at the Welcombe Hotel. Later, when the Welcombe had become too expensive, we slummed it at the Lygon Arms at Broadway, which was the better to explore the surrounding country. I longed to stay in the town itself and see the actors off-duty. I first went to Stratford in 1960 and have returned since for every season but one.

Recently, a mature American student asked me to give him a list of the best Shakespearean performances I had seen. I found that many came from the Stratford of my boyhood, and the spectacles were not tinted rose: Dorothy Tutin, husky-voiced, urgent and youthful as Viola and Portia - particularly the latter in a production (whose director Michael Langham I later besieged with questions) with designs based on Longhi, and a young, restrained, and dignified Peter O'Toole as Shylock. Max Adrian as Feste and Jacques, and - unbeaten since - Pandarus in *Troilus and Cressida*. (Later I came to know Max well and love him very much.) My mother loathed him as an actor, thinking him mannered and odd, while I thought him incisive, bold, and original.

She was a champion of Eric Porter, whose Malvolio, Macbeth, and Shylock I found emotionally cold. She was underwhelmed by Porter's Lady Macbeth, Irene Worth, whom I found unexpected and gripping (later her Volumnia was to be one of the very best of all Shakespearean performances that I've ever seen). We all disliked Christopher Plummer's Richard III ('that fool' pronounced Audry). Nor did we think much of little Miss Judi Dench, a bossy Isabella in *Measure for Measure.*

It was Vanessa Redgrave's Rosalind in *As You Like It* and Imogen in *Cymbeline* that seemed beyond praise in their wonder, beauty, vulnerability, and magnetism. And it was Paul Scofield's Timon of Athens that taught me what a great actor can make of a tricky text; I went over the lines in fine detail, remembering what his imagination had transmuted, what marvels he performed.

Audry's friend Norah Blaney (half of one of the first female comedy double-acts, Farrar and Blaney: Gwen Farrar, who also played the cello, and Norah, of concert standard on the piano) was in the company one year as a 'bitchy witch' in *Macbeth,* and Mistress Overdone in *Measure for Measure.* Norah objected to the lady's lavatories, newly installed backstage. From her shared dressing room, she said she could hear everything 'from first fart to final trickle'.

* * *

At the age of ten, I had also discovered opera, or at least opera from Mozart to Puccini, with Renata Tebaldi on the old Decca recording of *La Traviata*. My English opera-going matched in no way the glories of Salzburg, discovered at the same time, but Covent Garden became my favourite place in London, and I was an early Young Friend of Covent Garden. Early on there was Renata Scotto in *La Traviata* and *Il Trovatore*, as well as Klemperer conducting *Die Zauberflöte*, but it was Georg Solti's regime which, although it lacked the sheer splendour of Karajan's at Salzburg, had a fire and musicality that, in *The Ring*, *Otello*, and *Falstaff* in particular, were magnificent.

Going to the opera with my mother was sometimes hazardous. She had become enamoured of the barmaid at Covent Garden, who made the smoked salmon sandwiches in the old crush bar at the top of the great staircase. I knew the queers cruised where it split in two and became double, facing the wall-to-ceiling mirror. This lady was middle-aged, had no detectable attractions, and her beehived hair was bus-conductress black. Furthermore she seemed to have no interest or particular liking for my mother. 'What on earth do you find so special about her?' I asked snobbishly, both of us in evening dress at some first night.

'But she's so fascinating!' she cried. I was not allowed to accompany my mother when she approached this *femme fatale* for a sandwich, but I had to stand at the end of the bar in readiness to spring forward and carry the plate, if required. Somehow (I have no idea how) my mother managed to get a date and the two met somewhere. But I fear the meeting led to nothing, and from then on, if I wanted a sandwich, I had to go and ask for it myself.

CHAPTER EIGHT

TWO SCHOOLS

A lack of a normal family to surround me preyed on my mother's conscience, and so she selected for me a prep school run by what, on first meeting, she took to be that normal family. Cottesmore School, near Pease Pottage in Sussex, was an ugly Edwardian red sandstone building, at the centre of a large estate. Its attraction for Caroline was that her friends, the playwright and actor Emlyn Williams, and his wife Molly, had sent their sons there. Molly, pressed for an opinion, had said doubtfully, 'It's all right but it's very cold.' It was indeed cold. Very. And for four years I was always ill, riddled by colds followed by long periods of coughing my lungs out. The family who ran it were called Rogerson. The Headmaster was, and let no one forget it, a gentleman; his exceedingly dainty wife dressed from Harrods and their three children ranged from undergraduate to schoolboy.

It is fashionable for sensitive men of my generation and background to hate their prep schools, and such memories often make for boring reading, but I do think of Cottesmore as a bleak and loveless place where I was homesick, cold, miserable, and felt like a failure.

The first difficulty was that Mr. Rogerson disliked me on sight. I covered up the fact that I cried myself to sleep every night by a facade of cocky bravado. I talked about Vaynol and our guests, and in grand tones asked one of the masters who his wife had been before her marriage. I also struggled at work.

The Headmaster and his staff seemed baffled that I was so good at English, History and Divinity and so hopeless at Maths and languages. Plainly I was idle and needed to be punished. I was beaten, not for bad behaviour but, unforgivably, for ignorance. I was demoted to classes where there was no possibility of my strengths flourishing, while my incomprehension over arithmetic was not addressed; nor was any patience shown with my confusion.

It was probably not the only school of those days (or even perhaps these ones) which coped with the inadequacies of its teaching by sending its pupils on guilt-trips. Failure was rewarded by accusations of laziness and impertinence, and it was to be punished. At Cottesmore, this took the form of Rogerson beating boys on the bottom with an army swagger stick.

On the recommendation of Colonel Townend, Headmaster of Hill House, I had been placed in the second form. After a few days, Rogerson demoted me to the first, and I lost my confidence. Always the oldest in this and subsequent classes, and usually in the bottom few, concentration was a difficulty. Perhaps I was subconsciously attempting to process too much that was happening at home.

I also had a slight Welsh accent. It was known that I lived on a large estate, but that estate was clearly not in the South East of England, the only part of the world the other boys knew about. And in the South East I plainly did not belong.

Prep school masters were traditionally the dregs of the private teaching world, but Rogerson had found a truly woeful collection of paedophiles, psychopaths and losers.

His deputy, a man called Alan Hilder (a cousin of the artist Rowland) had been sacked from the staff of the public school at Lancing for his inability to control his temper. Resentful, faced with classes of younger boys, his rages were uncontrolled and very disturbing: hurling wooden-backed blackboard dusters that sometimes hit their mark, hitting about the head, and kicking personal property around the room. On my second day at the school, after I had said something to annoy him, he picked up the writing case that my mother had given me as a going-to-school present and tore it to pieces. When friendly, he would run his hand up the boys' shorts, pinch them very near their genitals, and stroke their buttocks. Rogerson was perfectly aware of all this activity and did nothing to curb it.

Another master, called Keeble-Williams, punched me so hard in the stomach for getting a question wrong in French that I feared I was seriously hurt. The next Sunday was an *exeat*, and I begged my mother to write him a note to say he couldn't do such things, and pleaded with her not to return me to a place where I was so frightened. But she said it 'wasn't done' to send masters notes and, if I tried harder and wasn't so lazy, masters would be kinder to me. Little boys needed to endure in order to become self-sufficient men.

Mr. Hobson, who taught Latin (although not to me, as I was too dumb for his attentions) and History (which I was good at) was so deranged that I found him quite fascinating, a real study in psychopathic lunacy. Because he recognized me as a fellow eccentric, he was comparatively benevolent to me. I learnt not to object if, when I was carrying a large pile of books, he banged my hands from underneath so the books flew all over the place, or if he squeezed my nose hard, or if he pulled the hairs at the back of my neck. A bright classicist and the youngest son of a parson, he must have been bullied by his elder brothers for he had, most surely, become a bully himself. As a policeman during the partition of India, he had doubtless seen dreadful sights and been ordered to impose brutal discipline, and this had tipped him over the edge. He twitched and had distressing tics: screwing his little finger into his ear while sucking in his cheeks. His rages were irrational and random, and his fear and hatred of the world and its inhabitants was pathetic. He used to hide from parents, whom he never dared face, let alone speak to.

The matron, who was meant to minister to our afflictions, which were usually brought on by cold and terror, was known as 'Nurse'. She was a woman with a low level of compassion. Dressed with a napkin on her head like a nurse in the First World War, any boy who said 'Nurse, I don't feel well,' was rewarded with, 'You wouldn't, would you?' Anything that inconvenienced her brought out her foul temper. Little boys who wet their beds or worse were screamed at. How I rejoiced when someone was sick on the floor during the night and she had to clean it up (in the daytime she had an assistant matron for those purposes). Once, when I was in bed, stone-deaf and shivering with 'flu, my mother came to see me, bringing a bottle of Ribena. It was a present that I never received, because Nurse stole it and was seen slurping it down with her sidekick in the corridor. An older boy, who had never before been particularly friendly, advised me to tell my mother. But what was the point?

I was thrown from a horse at full gallop during the rehearsal for Sport's Day. My foot was caught twisted in the stirrup and I was dragged along the ground, being kicked in the stomach and face as the horse continued to race. I could have been dying, but Nurse, doubtless fearful she might not be able to cope, just angrily told me that it was my fault because I had been wearing the wrong riding boots.

It was at Cottesmore, however, that something deep inside me responded to the ill treatment and poor teaching. In spite of my idiocy, I knew I wanted to teach, and teach very differently from the bullies and fools I had encountered there. Furthermore, I knew I wanted to teach at a more advanced level. I told this to the only decent human being on the staff, a Welshman called Roberts, a mathematician who for one term only had taught me fractions (a skill I still have, although it is quite useless in a decimal age). He said he thought that one day I would do just that. I felt astonished and tearful at his reaction, whether sincere or not. It was very different from the Headmaster and Hobson, who had, in front of the entire school, drawn attention to a letter received from Sir John Wolfenden, a recent friend of my mother's (Chancellor of Reading University and author of the famous report, for Heaven's sake), suggesting I took a scholarship to my public school because my strengths might be considered over my weaknesses. They all laughed at the absurdity of the idea.

I played Shylock in the trial scene from *The Merchant of Venice*. This brought me some acclaim, although the tin-legged English master who directed, and who had previously seemed to see some imagination in my essays, took against me hurtfully and unaccountably the following term. He joined the club of masters bent on my humiliation.

Letters home were written twice a week and censored; no complaints allowed. 'We don't want you saying that,' said Rogerson. All the other boys seemed to start theirs 'Dear Daddy and Mummy'. But not me. Letters had to be written to my mother alone, and as she held it common to address a relation as 'dear', they had to start, 'Darling Mummy', which caused mirth from anybody who looked over my shoulder. With these sons of prosperous Sussex businessmen and men of the professions, I was howlingly embarrassed by my mother's title. Nor did 'Lady Caroline Duff' suffice. It had to be '*The* Lady Caroline Duff' or back came the envelope, corrected. One boy, the grandson of a baron, thought my mother, as a baronet's wife, ought to be just 'Lady Duff'. 'You are insulting my grandfather,' he said, and threatened to beat me up if he saw an envelope mistitled again. He did so, and, unbelievably, his parents complained to the Headmaster. When told that my mother was a Marquess's sister, the same boy came up and said that his parents would like me to tea one Sunday. The invitation was refused.

As always, I felt like a misfit amongst the many, but was able to have close friendships with a few. But these friendships became strained for I never reciprocated the hospitality that my friends' parents gave me, since I was so embarrassed by mine. My mother came to most events with Audry. Who was she, I was asked by masters and boys? An aunt? 'No, a friend of my mother's.' Occasionally Michael would appear and it must have been fairly obvious that I was not his son. One Sports Day, fathers and sons had a three-legged race that my mother captured on her cine-camera. Even today I wince when watching it. He had no idea what was meant to happen in a three-legged race, and we repeatedly fell over. It was the cause of great hilarity to the assembled parents, staff and boys. We came last.

'Why did you never ask anyone home?' asked my mother years later. 'Wasn't it the sort of home you felt you could ask anyone to?'

Surely she knew the answer.

In those days, boys like me, bound for Eton, took their Common Entrance examination at twelve, while the other public schools held the exam at thirteen. I was the only boy due to go to Eton. I took my examination in the fourth form, when the Common Entrance form was the fifth. The terror I felt for the whole year before undertaking this certain failure undermined me for a long time.

When the news of my failure was received, Rogerson summoned me to his study and shouted at me, purple in the face: 'You have let your mother down, you have let your father down...' I was brave enough to tell him that I had warned my mother I would fail, because my plea for the exam to be postponed a year had been ignored by him. 'You will take your Common Entrance when I say so!'

My mother's reaction shocked me more. She came to the school and walked me round and round the playing fields berating me and panicking. 'What's to happen to us now?'

'But I warned you I would fail.'

'I didn't believe you.'

I was twelve, but I understood that I was being blamed by grown-ups for their own misjudgements. I knew my mother really minded - not for me, but because it reflected badly on her.

It was never the same between us after that. The dear little boy was becoming a man and I think that repelled the lesbian in her.

Matters were certainly not going to plan.

* * *

Two joys, however, did arise from my failure. The first was that Caroline removed me from that hated place. The second was that she found a small school for me to attend for a year, as different to Cottesmore in spirit and in atmosphere as could be imagined.

Frensham Manor was near Rolvenden in my favourite English county, Kent, where I have not spent a single unhappy day. It was a house of real beauty - in part medieval - and it housed a small school of perhaps thirty boys, who were not good at their studies. This time the family who lived there were a delight, relaxed, happy, and fun.

The Reverend Brian Kirk-Duncan, 'The Rector' to us, was incumbent of the parish St. Mary-at-Hill in the City of London. It included the Billingsgate fish market, to which he was chaplain. After teaching us divinity with great humour and charm every morning before breakfast, he departed in a blue Rolls-Royce to his daily ministry in

London, leaving us in the care of his deputy, a young man just down from Cambridge called Guy Nelder. There was a collection of masters, retired from other schools, old men who had fought in the First World War.

The Rector's wife Quita had the kindest and most humorous face. Life for her, if not a joy, was an endless opportunity to show kindness and to laugh at trouble. She relished being in place of our mothers. Her house was one of warmth, where people enjoyed themselves and respected each other.

The Rector was no pushover. He was quite strict and brooked no nonsense. But he fostered an atmosphere where the installation of self-belief was paramount. He knew that unless people feel good about themselves, they are unlikely to learn anything.

Guy Nelder seemed like the older brother and mentor I had never had. A slightly built young man, he was a brilliant historian, a teacher of much verve and imagination. He was also irreverent, sophisticated, very heterosexual and always full of gusto and life. He seemed to love our company, but his authority was effortless and absolute, and no one played him up. He saw that my love of history was passionate and true, and he openly hoped that I might one day win a History scholarship to Cambridge. Never before, ever, had anyone held out such hopes for me.

Teaching Latin and Geography was Mr. Catleigh, once a housemaster at Repton, a man in his seventies who told us vivid stories of the trenches and the cold that made him cry with misery. He was not an admirer of the aristocracy, he confessed, but liked me, as I certainly did him, and I responded to his hugely experienced and excellent teaching.

French and English were taught by Reverend Wilfrid Oldaker, erstwhile don of Christ Church and then Headmaster of the prep school of King's School, Canterbury. He was a small roly-poly man. 'A dirty boy has made a dirty smell, and dirty boys have dirty characters,' he announced when someone ('not me, sir') farted. He taught us Christian Darwinism, which has always seemed sensible to me, and directed us in James Bridie's *Tobias and the Angel*. I played Raphael, an archangel with whom I have always since felt a connection, because he is the great healer, and because he has the best sense of humour of all the company of Heaven.

For that enterprise, Mrs. Oldaker, whose two feet were encased in surgical boots and whose merry apple-cheeked face was surrounded by plaited headphones of hair, made the lovely costumes with her own fair hands. The Oldakers looked like Mr. and Mrs. Noah from a toy wooden Ark.

Colonel Troupe, who owned a mink farm, taught maths. 'Duff,' he exhorted, 'Kindly drag your mind away from Russian ballet and return it to algebra.' At that age I had never given Russian ballet a single thought in my life.

Guy Nelder taught History with a sweeping narrative drive. He also read us Conan Doyle's *The White*

Company and Josephine Tey's excellent historical novel on Viscount Dundee, *Claverhouse*.

The Rector mistrusted games and, after one desultory attempt at a football match, we just went for walks in the afternoon, and in the summer sat around and swam in the pool, which was a luxurious addition to the house.

We worked, although none of us ever felt under any pressure, and we all passed our exams. The Rector thought that Eton was a silly school for me to attend, and suggested Bryanston as an alternative, where it was hoped my acting and music might flourish. It had the added advantage of being close to my grandmother Juliet at Bulbridge.

* * *

Forty years later, I was happy to seek out the Rector, then in his eighties and still the vicar of St. Mary-at-Hill, to thank him. He asked me to read a lesson at his Wednesday service. When I told him that my overriding defect of character was impatience, he said, 'Patience is a virtue, virtue is a grace, and Grace is a little girl who wouldn't wash her face!' At his memorial service a few years later, some of my letter of condolence to Quita was read out by his son Anthony. I had written that he had confirmed to me that the basis of all good teaching is kindness and the instilling of self-belief.

CHAPTER NINE

VAYNOL AGAIN: GENDER BENDING

One autumn in the early 1960s, Aunt Veronica, sitting at home in Tangier with her booze, cigarettes and emphysema, heard something that greatly displeased her. David Stuart, the new estate manager, intended to attempt to break the entail created by Michael's grandfather, Sir Charles Assheton-Smith. It stipulated that Vaynol had to pass to his blood descendants. David's purpose was practical: money would be released to pay off the estate's debts, and the estate could then be left to me, who considered it home. Veronica and her children were to be offered a lump sum in lieu of an inheritance, and a letter was sent to Tangier to find out if this arrangement might be acceptable.

It was not.

Veronica arrived at Vaynol just before the Christmas holidays. My mother came to collect me from school with the news that there had been a serious accident. Daddy had somehow fallen over the banisters of the main staircase, from a height of about twelve feet, dislocating his shoulder and injuring his neck. How this had happened was a mystery, but he was very lucky indeed not to be more seriously hurt.

We arrived at Vaynol to find brother and sister alone together: Veronica, tottering about with glass in hand, and Michael, strapped up and clearly in pain.

The story, by now being told as an amusing anecdote, was that the two were coming down before dinner, when Michael had 'suddenly disappeared' over the side of the staircase.

'That sounds very puzzling,' said my mother dryly. It took no great leap of the imagination to conclude that there had been a drunken quarrel upstairs in my father's study and, coming downstairs together, Veronica had pushed him over the banisters.

'If it's so important to her for her lot to have it that she's prepared to stoop to fratricide [I knew my Cain and Abel and my *Hamlet*] I think I'd rather let them take it and go and live elsewhere,' I said.

'Yes, quite!' replied my mother.

Very occasionally my father had shown interest in women in his youth. The one to whom he lost his virginity was the easy-going and interesting daughter of Edward VII's mistress, Mrs. Keppel. She was called Sonia Cubitt, and she had a granddaughter called Camilla Shand - now Duchess of Cornwall. She had a hooked nose, a long neck, talked a lot and was very funny. I remember to this day her imitation of Sir Oswald Mosley trying to seduce her.

I felt quite at ease with Sonia and looked forward to her frequent visits, as I did the annual two-week stay of Dorothy Dickson, as she made her progress around various country houses. Her glamour and delicious smell delighted me. She appears in a cine-film of my mother's, and her clothes and her movement are so gorgeous. I longed to ask her about Ivor Novello and Drury Lane and her Peter Pan, where she flew more beautifully than anyone. But Dottie had erased her past. It made her seem too old, and anyway she had given it all up. Many years later, when the director Frith Banbury asked her to be in a revival of *Dear Octopus* with her contemporaries Cicely Courtneidge and Jack Hulbert, she said, 'Oh, I couldn't appear with those old has-beens!' Dottie was a devout Christian Scientist and had great integrity and moral bearing. Once I spent the day alone with her, and I loved the grace and courtesy she showed to a boring schoolboy.

Also brought up as a Christian Scientist by her great-aunt Nancy, Lady Astor, was my very favourite of all the Vaynol guests, Elizabeth Winn. She was the 'E. Winn' of so many country-house memoirs, decorator of class and beauty, lover of chamber music and jazz. Elizabeth was a child herself, in the best sense of the word, so full of fun, ready to join in any jaunt, enter into every game or adventure. She was what Dilys the housemaid called 'a scream'. Private, celibate and contained in her personal life, in friendship she was all warmth, wit, taste and delight.

* * *

On my early morning expeditions, I would steal a fistful of cigarettes from one of the numerous boxes lying around downstairs, go out of the courtyard door when it was still dark, and run to my hut in the woods - Charley's Woods - where I smoked, thought, and sang arias from Verdi operas as the sun rose. Apparently I could be heard from the house a quarter of a mile away.

I was aware that I was not the son that my father wanted. I understood that he wanted a son with all the attributes I lacked: unconventional elegance, an eccentric taste in clothes, a love of parties, a knowledge of furniture and antiques and, most importantly, someone who was sought after by others.

The first of his surrogate sons was a bit of a failure. He was a Hungarian student, who after the revolution of 1956 had been befriended and helped by my father's Hungarian friend Miki Sekers. Michael de Szell, this wholly pleasant and gentle young man, was studying design at Aberystwyth University, from whence he came to stay most weekends. He did not own a dressing gown and I remember us taking him into Bangor to buy one. My father soon tired of him and he rather disappeared. But happily he made a great success of his life as a designer of textiles and beautiful materials, which he sold to the grand and the Royal who had become his friends. Whenever I met him in later life, I sensed in him the loveliest energy. However, he was a great fantasist. I never knew how much of what he said was the truth, and he certainly told a lot of fibs about his relationship with my father. He said he was his adopted son, which caused me some embarrassment later on, because I never wanted to belittle him by refuting the claim.

The artist Patrick Procktor, however, was far more Michael's son than I ever was. He even looked exactly like him: excessively tall, with a look of permanent wide-eyed astonishment. He modelled himself on Michael and, after my father's death, it was always most unsettling for me to meet Michael's reincarnation when I was trying so hard to exorcise his ghost. He wore strange clothes topped by a fez, and imitated Michael's vocabulary, delivery, and even his stutter. Their relationship was, however, a fruitful one. Vaynol provided Patrick with a place where he could paint unbothered, and their holidays together, to Tangier or Venice, were great fun, and furthermore had some real purpose, because Patrick was always painting. Patrick's great friend then was David Hockney. But while Hockney was to become the pre-eminent British artist of his time, Patrick's reputation has not really flourished. I believe his work to possess considerable stature and beauty, but perhaps he was a bit too impressed by Vaynol and its life and the people like Cecil Beaton, to whom Michael introduced him. In return, Patrick's success brought Michael into contact with trendy swinging London. My father was genuinely fond of Patrick and would have been sad to see him become so disappointed in the latter years of his life.

* * *

In the sixties, Vaynol was still run as formally as any pre-war country house, with a staff of nine for a resident family of three. My mother would spend a long time making out the places at dinner on a leather board the same shape as the dining room table, and on the first night of a house party, guests sat in order of precedence (Duchesses on my father's right, for instance). At Wilton they stayed in order of precedence all weekend!

My mother's cutlery was smaller than that of the guests, because she thought the *nouveaux riches* Assheton-Smiths' big knives and forks were common.

Before dinner, Edward Howes, wearing the most beautiful cream shirt and linen dinner jacket in summer, and tails in winter, offered guests the White Ladies, for which he was famous. But those guests were rarely in straightforward evening dress. Eccentricity was encouraged. Anything unusual or outlandish was welcomed. Convention was considered dull. Seated around the dining-room table in the candlelight and the gleam of the silver, when the lights had been switched off after the pudding, the guests sometimes looked like creatures from a Fellini film, in their strange and exotic clothes: surreal and weird.

Men appeared dressed as women. Hugh Cruddas often came as the Queen Mother, for instance, and Edward would say, poker-faced, 'A cocktail, Your Majesty?' I entered into this spirit but with no real enthusiasm, and my father despised me for lacking it. I found it lacking any real humour or joy. It was somehow forced. Too many of these people put on silly fancy dress because they lacked any true individuality. Sometimes, I suspected they just wanted to fit in and play my father's game.

Dress was more conventional when Royalty was present.

But Vaynol as a house, as an institution, was about to be blasted apart, and blasted apart by me.

CHAPTER TEN

BECOMING A WAGNERIAN

One winter afternoon my mother and I drove over to Plas Newydd to see her brother and my cousins. As we walked through the house with its strong smell of incense, I heard the most thrilling sound, something beyond any experience I had ever had. That sound resonated in me so deeply that it blew me away.

As we entered the saloon (as the drawing room was called there) my uncle Henry was miming cracking a double-handed whip, while his children ran around screaming. He was playing Alberich, they the *Nibelungen* dwarves, forging the ring and the *tarnhelm*.

The Decca recording of *Das Rheingold* conducted by Georg Solti had just been released. Henry's gramophone was the best and loudest that the world could then offer, and the sound that filled the huge room, and that rhythm (di di di da-da-da, di di di da-da-da, as the anvils are hammered) was the most theatrical, thrilling and visceral thing I had ever heard. That music, which is just scene-change cover as the action shifts from the earth to Nibelheim, still thrills me as no other. I had become a Wagnerian.

With Christmas money, I bought two records: Klemperer conducting The Apprentices' Dance from

Die Meistersinger and Siegfried's Funeral March, and my mother's old pin-up, Hans Knappertsbusch, conducting various orchestral highlights. Over time my collection grew and I played it loud.

The house shook. My playroom was just above the butler's pantry, where Edward Howes worked. How he stood for it I don't know, because I played favoured tracks over and over again. It was a drug, which took me to forbidden depths, lifted me to ecstatic heights, and propelled me into euphoria. Why did nobody try to dissuade me from what was becoming an unbalanced obsession rather than a real hobby? My father said nothing until he decided to take action - but that action was quite simple. He took over my playroom while I was at school, threw most of my books and records away (he did this quite regularly), and turned the room into an office without telling me. My portable gramophone and I were banished to my bedroom on the top floor. I doubt that anybody other than myself was displeased.

* * *

This newly converted Wagnerian was just thirteen. At the end of those holidays, I was sitting downstairs at Paultons Square looking through some Temple editions of Shakespeare. Along with the small bookshelf where they lived, these are the only pieces of Audry Carten's estate that I now possess. I found a book of poems in my mother's writing. They were love poems and quite sexual, describing nights of passion - many, it seemed, on a night sleeper from Holyhead to Euston. In case I was confused there was a dedication: 'To Audry, from *her* Caroline.' It was a bolt of recognition. The missing piece of the jigsaw slotted into place. *That* was what it was all about. *That* was what our cook meant when I overheard her telling Moussia that it was disgraceful how my mother and Miss Carten lay in bed together for all to see, and how was I going to grow up, living in such an atmosphere? *That* was what it was about when Audry and my mother kissed on the mouth when we left Paultons Square. And why, when the three of us went on holiday together, my mother sometimes dressed more like a man than a woman. And indeed, why my parents were hardly a conventional couple.

I was slightly disturbed; but only slightly. I sensed it was unnatural, but I loved neither my mother nor Audry less for the discovery. It made me understand, despite my sadness, why my mother put her first, before me, before all. My understanding was to be required very shortly: premature senility struck Audry with all its degrading concomitants, terror, and incontinence, when she was only in her early sixties.

CHAPTER ELEVEN

TWO CONDUCTORS

We spent many holidays in Austria, both in winter, for skiing, and in summer, for music. We stayed at my aunt Liz von Hofmannsthal's house, a small mediaeval castle called Schloss Prielau. My father never came with us. Liz was the most beautiful of my mother's sisters, tall and dark with grave brown eyes inherited from her mother. She should have been painted by Ingres, for she had such poise and grace, both of body and mind. She was also my godmother. She was deeply musical, with a privileged access to musicians and their world. At Prielau there was no television or radio. Instead, music was played every night on what was, for those times, a gloriously fine gramophone. It was there that I heard and learnt much of the German symphonic and operatic repertoire.

Liz's husband Raimund was the son of Richard Strauss's librettist, Hugo von Hofmannsthal, and he was the most worldly and civilized man that I have ever met; almost entirely without rancour or adverse judgement of others. He combined a sensualist's appreciation of all the pleasures of life with an almost innocent good nature and a belief in the inherent goodness of humanity. He had a charm which seemed

to come from a *belle époque*, an earlier and more benevolent age. He was attuned to my adolescent sadness,
approved of me and found me interesting, and I loved
him a lot for that. 'Don't worry about not having a
relationship with your father,' he reassured me in Vi-
ennese-sounding English, 'because nobody does. Not
your mother. Nobody. And if you need anything come
to me.' He also admonished, 'Don't treat your mother
like that! She's an old lady. She's even older than Liz!'
Both women were in their early fifties.

Like many famously beautiful women, Liz had great
insecurities. She feared that she was dull and uneducated, and I always suspected, although I could never
fathom why, that she was unhappy. She seemed so
exactly like the Countess in her beloved *Figaro,* or
the Marschallin in her father-in-law's *Der Rosenkavalier;* for Raimund had a roving eye, although he was
good-mannered about his conduct, and I was unaware
of the existence of his mistress until after his death.

Their son Octavian was three years older than me,
and although we fought constantly, he was the nearest
thing I had to a brother. His sister Arabella, three years
older than he, had a difficult relationship with her
mother but was as sweet-natured as her father, and as
part of emerging Swinging London, seemed incredibly
with-it and trendy. Both my parents adored her.

Prielau was a concise box-like castle, inside all bare
floorboards and porcelain stoves with seats round
them, where people sat to warm their backs. The

guests were cosmopolitan, although Liz's family and Raimund's daughters by his first marriage to Alice Astor were the most constant, as well as an enchanting aunt of his called Marianne, who lived in New York. Once we arrived with Liz as the house was opened up before Christmas, and the servants lined up outside and kissed the adults' hands, as if in a Russian novel.

Raimund's mother Gertie, the great man's widow, seemed rather an ordinary *hausfrau*. Perhaps her ordinariness had helped and balanced that introspective and pained artist. 'Look at zeeze two boys, zey are such friends!' she beamed as Octavian and I, dishevelled and glaring at each other, disentangled ourselves from a fight. After the war, during the first broadcast of her husband's collaborator's *Four Last Songs*, all her family sat enraptured around the wireless when Flagstad sang *Beim schlafengehen*. Then Gertie suddenly sprung up and announced, 'Ach, I must anuzzer egg in ze pudding put!'

It was at Prielau that my mother had an argument with Martha Gellhorn, the famous war correspondent and former wife of Ernest Hemingway. I found Miss Gellhorn (then and later) charmless and aggressive. She had adopted a boy of my age from an Italian orphanage. Forced to go out on the ski slopes together, this child and I loathed each other. I found him brattish, rude and hostile. I had been told that on no account was I to refer to his adoption, as his mother was not going to tell him. My mother thought this iniquitous and said so, and the two women had a very heated argument in *Mosshammer's*, the café in town, where we all gathered. This young man and his adoptive mother were to appear in my life again.

The glory of Prielau for me was that it was near Salzburg and its music festival, the most prestigious in Europe, which Hugo von Hofmannsthal had co-founded. I fell for beautiful Salzburg, with its castle on high and its cathedral, as I have for no other city. My festival-going years spanned the sixties, so I saw Herbert von Karajan's *régime* there at its height. Doubtless it was expensive and elitist. It was certainly international and glamorous. When his arrogance and cold calculation were not reflected in his music, Karajan was the greatest conductor I have heard, the one who gave me the most distinguished and beautiful musical experiences of my life.

And the casts! Eberhard Waechter, Elisabeth Schwarzkopf, and Leontyne Price in a *Don Giovanni* produced by Oscar Fritz Schuh, the only one I have seen where the comedy and drama were really successfully married. And at the Large Festspielhaus, I saw an *Il Trovatore* with Leontyne Price ('the most beautiful voice in the world' said Karajan, at a time when colour-blind casting was not to be found elsewhere), Franco Corelli, Giulietta Simionato and the dying Ettore Bastianini; *Boris Godunov* with Nicolai Ghiaurov and Sena Jurinac; *Elektra* with Astrid Varnay, and *The Ring*, particularly the *Siegfried,* with

Jess Thomas and a young Helga Dernesch. When the Easter Festival began there was a *Haydn Creation* and a Bruckner Eighth, when I sat just behind the conductor. And of course, every summer in front of the Cathedral there was Hofmannsthal's play *Jedermann*, still in Max Reinhardt's production, now rehearsed by his son Gottfried.

As a producer, Karajan was rather decried, but I saw his productions (greatly influenced by Gordon Craig and Adolphe Appia) on the then-biggest stage in the world, the Large Fetspielhaus, and I found them brooding and magnificent and have never forgotten them.

Raimund and Liz knew Herbert and Eliette von Karajan, both through the Festival and because Eliette had once 'walked out' with Liz and my mother's cousin the Duke of Rutland. Their first visit to Prielau was rather frightening. Octavian and I touched Karajan's extremely snazzy new sports car and he shouted 'Get your hands off!' in his rasping voice. We at once christened him 'Adolf' - long before we knew of his supposed Nazi affiliations.

I was alone with my mother and Liz one summer when Eliette asked herself to stay for a few days, while Herbert and the Vienna Philharmonic were at the Edinburgh Festival. Younger than her husband, French, and casually elegant, she laughed frequently and joyously, and I found her a complete delight. She pronounced her husband's name as if he were French. Trying to be sophisticated, I asked, 'And does *Airbair*

conduct much Wagner?' which embarrassed Liz and
my mother, but made Eliette scream with laughter. She
asked whether I would like one of *Airbair*'s batons,
which of course I did, and one was later sent. I sent
my thank-you letter to the wrong address, so it looked
as if I were unappreciative, which was certainly not
the case. But I felt I was never quite forgiven for the
solecism.

With the conductor, I had a far less happy time.
In April 1963, Raimund and Liz dragged me along
uninvited for a late-night supper at the Connaught
Hotel, just after he had conducted the First and Ninth
Beethoven Symphonies at the Festival Hall. He was
plainly displeased that I was there and took no notice
of me. He had spent the morning watching Princess
Alexandra's wedding on television, and said that only
the English could produce such pomp and specta-
cle. He boasted that his recent recording of *Tosca* in
Vienna with Leontyne Price was quite wonderful, and
that Giuseppe di Stefano was singing at his best again.
But he became bad-tempered and sulky when Liz said
she had hated the Paul Czinner film of *Der Rosenkavalier*, with 'Schwarzkopf's black lipstick', which he
had conducted.

I thought he had not registered me at all, so I was
surprised when, about a year later, he and Eliette were
dining at the Hofmannsthals' London house, and he
was charm itself: he said how much I had grown,
sat on the sofa beside me and focused his complete

attention on this teenage boy, as the others listened. I asked him about televised opera, and said how bad a recent *Aida* from the Verona Arena had been, with the tenor singing in the wrong key all the way through *Celeste Aida*. 'But that aria is very difficult; it is set low for the tenor voice, and comes near the start of the opera. What happened is understandable.' I asked him about the forthcoming *Boris Godunov* at Salzburg. Why was he using Rimsky-Korsakov's orchestration rather than Mussorgsky's original one? 'Only because it is a large theatre,' he replied. 'The original would sound too thin there. It's a wonderful acoustic, but a big, big space. We will need that sumptuousness, and also a choir that can sing Russian. We are borrowing one, all a hundred of them, from Sofia.'

He also told me: 'The worst experience I ever had was in Vienna conducting *Parsifal*. I swatted a fly and the woodwind section came in five bars too early. Within seconds there was chaos. I had to stop the whole orchestra completely and bring in each section one at a time until we were back on course. On stage everyone had frozen.'

On Herbert's arrival at the London house, Raimund had presented him with a facsimile of the original libretto of *Der Rosenkavalier*, which he had kissed and clasped to his heart - only to leave it behind when he left!

Karajan had a sidekick and dogsbody called André von Mattoni. Baron Mattoni was a well-dressed, slick, feline queen, who took against me intransigently and

Michael and Caroline's wedding day by Cecil Beaton.
© The Cecil Beaton Studio Archive at Sotheby's.

VAYNOL

Charley and Caroline by Cecil Beaton. © The Cecil Beaton Studio Archive at Sotheby's.

Charley in Caroline's bed at Vaynol by Cecil Beaton. © The Cecil Beaton Studio Archive at Sotheby's.

Caroline.

Her partner
Audry Carten.

Opposite:
Caroline and
Charley at a
wedding in
London.

Above: Bridget Paget (left), Angelica Weldon and Angus Menzies at Vaynol.

Left: Irene Carisbrooke and Charley.

Above: Michael and Charley at Red Wharf bay.

Below: Charley and Caroline on the shores of the Menai Straits.

Above left: Irene Carisbrooke

Above right: Drino Carisbrooke (right) appreciates Andy Tennant (left).

Above left: Louisa Farrell and Charley at Vaynol.

Above right: Simon Fleet with his tapestry.

Right: My
grandmother Juliet
with Simon Fleet.

Below:
Marguerite McBey.

Above: Caroline at Llyn Dywarchen with Snowdon in the background by Cecil Beaton. © The Cecil Beaton Studio Archive at Sotheby's.

Opposite above: Caroline (left), Cecil Beaton and Princess Marina at Llyn Dywarchen.

Opposite below: Caroline holding Charley and Michael.

Above:
Caroline (left),
Diana Cooper
and Liz von
Hofmannsthal
with Doggie
at Warwick
Avenue.

Left: Caroline
and Charley
at Marguerite
McBey's sea
house in
Tangier.

Charley at
the age of
seventeen.

Schloss
Prielau.

Opposite: Neville Clarke (Tom Clark), *en grande tenue.*

Mary Letitia Orpen, descended from Charlemagne, married to a gamekeeper.

David Gray.

The Grays at
Rockcorry after
Dunmanway: (left to
right) Evelyn, Walter,
Alice, Reggie and
Irene.

Irene Gray (right)
with her sister-in-
law, Barbara.

with vigour when I informed him, over and over again during a dinner in Salzburg at the *Goldener Hirsch*, that London was the music capital of the world and that British orchestras were the best. My chauvinism was meant to annoy him and it clearly did, and it did not endear me to his master either. I assume news of my bumptiousness was passed on, because shortly after, an invitation I had received to attend a rehearsal of a Brahms concert was withdrawn. How extraordinary that Karajan thought my immature opinion was a threat, or that it even mattered. But the message had registered that the Karajans were angry, and this slight was meant to punish me. I have since put it down to a certain social chippiness that Karajan carried over from his youth; whether because he was small, or because his first wife's family had looked down on him, who knows? Raimund and Liz, also invited, did not attend the rehearsal in support of me, and I don't think they ever saw either of the Karajans again.

* * *

Sir Thomas Beecham called Karajan 'a sort of musical Malcolm Sargent', but I think Karajan and Sargent had only met once, early in the war in Stockholm. Karajan had taken pleasure in telling Sargent, 'When the Fuhrer conquers London, you will be shot.'

'Thank-you,' Sargent had replied. 'How gratifying to be on the wanted list of the SS.'

Malcolm Sargent had been a boyfriend of my mother's. 'Well, he makes a pass at anything in a skirt!' she said. My godfather David Herbert used to tell people that Sargent was my father (presumably because I pretended to conduct records with Karajan's stick). I certainly loved Malcolm and I only wish that he had been my father. But I fear he wasn't.

The 'Flash Harry' aspect of Sargent - the brilliantined hair and the air of self-conscious elegance, the spivishness that made him not quite a gentleman - is rather mocked now, and there is a belief that his conducting was superficial and rather cheap. Yet Toscanini called him the greatest choral conductor in the world, and he was. English music owes him an incalculable debt. At his best, in the great choral works such as Elgar's *The Dream of Gerontius*, he was sovereign. Even his Handel and Haydn, dated and Victorian to our ears, are so expressive and profound. He brought classical music to hundreds of thousands through radio, as the chief conductor of the B.B.C. Symphony Orchestra, and to thousands of children through the Mayer-Sargent Children's Concerts. They were the first concerts I went to, and although he did not conduct, Malcolm had sent us the tickets. He threw himself into every performance with absolute emotional commitment; I saw him sometimes befuddled with psychic exhaustion after a concert.

I first met him backstage at the Albert Hall after the penultimate night of the Proms, when he had conducted Beethoven's Ninth. We had gone back to his flat in

Albert Hall Mansions opposite, where he was charming and sweet and made me feel important. I was carrying a pocket score and he reacted with mock-horror: 'I hope you are not planning to conduct this!'

Malcolm was always surrounded by beautiful girls. He had one on each arm when he went to the theatre. I once saw him and his harem arriving late; rather than disturb the rest of the audience, they all sat on the floor until the interval, which I thought, and still think, excellent manners. He was truly wonderful with children, ruffling hair and pinching cheeks, habits that are usually anathema, but which from him were a privilege received.

The greatest treat that came from my mother's friendship with Malcolm was going to a rehearsal of the Last Night of the Proms. My mother and I were the only ones in the whole hall singing *Land of Hope and Glory* and the chorus of his own arrangement of *Rule Britannia*! The television producer kept telling the contralto Constance Shacklock to stand in a different place, much to her confusion, and there was a lot of laughter, as there should be at a rehearsal. But Malcolm gave the young organist a very hard time. Conductors, in my experience, are never wholly pleasant.

CHAPTER TWELVE

GREEK TRAGEDY
PERSONIFIED

The musical paths of Maria Callas and Malcolm Sargent crossed only once, I think, when Malcolm introduced her on a television programme, flinging his arms wide: 'The great Callas!' He then accompanied her on the piano in *Tu che le vanità* from *Don Carlo* and *L'altra notte* from *Mefistofele* (rather badly - it was not his *fach*, as the Germans say).

Callas's voice fascinated me from the moment I heard her sing Gilda in *Rigoletto* on record. There was no other voice like it: dark, primal, and intense, with a musicality and dramatic intelligence that were faultless. (What a wonderful gospel singer she would have made!) It was the only voice of which I could never hear enough and never tire. 'How can you bear those screeches and wobbles?' teased Elizabeth Winn. 'I could do better!'

'Callas wrecks the opera every time she opens her mouth,' said Aunt Liz, listening to a *Lucia* recording. But I have always found, as the philosopher Bacon said, that 'There is no excellent beauty that hath not some strangeness in the proportion.' Callas's voice had hooked me as does a drug. The metallic edge and un-controlled spread of some notes above the stave were to me all part of the expressiveness, the musical artic-ulation. Even at the end of her career, when her vocal problems were serious, she could communicate as no other performer - not just as no other *singer* - has ever been able to do. Sutherland and Caballé, with their dazzling technical perfection, could impress but never really interest me. One of *Airbair*'s passports to my affection was that he revered her and swore (not quite truthfully) that working with her had never given him a second's trouble.

She was such a subject for conversation. Had her famous loss of weight had a deleterious effect on her voice? Had she swallowed a tapeworm? Her clothes, her temperament, her glamorous life on Onassis's yacht, and her (by then very occasional) appearanc-es as Norma or Medea, which almost caused riots, all made her the absolute world *diva* in my eyes: an apotheosis of the performing artist.

Certainly she had, and has, a huge gay following. But no one could claim that those other fag icons, Judy Garland, Edith Piaf, or Madonna, could com-municate such profound feelings or tell such great truths about our grief, our struggles, our courage and our nobility. She was, as a colleague of hers remarked, Greek tragedy personified.

My mother saw her first, in concert, and wrote to me while I was at school to report that even when she was standing still, it was clear she was the actress of the century. Her vocal deficiencies were immaterial to the complete experience. Then she and Audry went to the famous 1964 *Tosca* (the broadcast of which I listened to at school, under the bedclothes). My mother said her magic on stage was such that she knew that there would never be another Tosca like her. However Audry, who had worshipped Maria Jeritza, lying prone for *Vissi d'Arte* in days long gone, thought her femininity idiotic: 'She played Tosca like a little girl!'

That May, it was announced that she would sing her greatest role, Norma, at the Paris Opera, in a new production by Franco Zeffirelli. My mother, realising that this might be my only chance of seeing this extraordinary artist, decided to splash out for my half-term with an extravagance she had never shown before. It was for me, at fourteen, a rite of passage: musical, dramatic and sensual (it was my first visit to Paris). It was one of the highlights of my life, by which I have ever since judged all expeditions, and usually found them wanting.

Diana Cooper (once Ambassadress in Paris) was roped in, and she asked Georges Auric, director of *L'Opéra,* to help. He sent us two of the best seats.

On the day of the half-term break we were driven by George the chauffeur - whom my mother had never before commandeered for herself - from Bulbridge, my grandmother's house, to London Airport (as Heathrow was then known). The aeroplane (as they were then called) took us to Paris where we were met by a glamorous, young, rich, gay couple, whom my mother somehow knew. They took us to the Ritz, where we were staying (wow! I still have the photographs), and then for a day's sightseeing, before dinner at Maxim's, and later, my first visit to a nightclub.

The next day, Saturday, was the day of the performance, and Diana Cooper's old secretary called us with alarming news. Callas had missed a top note earlier in the week and been booed. Had she walked off stage? Or had she stopped the orchestra and sung the phrase again? No one seemed sure. Diana's secretary had heard from someone who knew her that Madame Callas had dangerously low blood pressure, and would cry off appearing again. Don't be disappointed if that is the case, warned my mother. Don't be disappointed!

The Salle Garnier was the most ornate and opulent building I had ever seen. I had been studying its ground plan and elevations in a book, and was overwhelmed by the complexity and excessive beauty of its design (no strangeness of proportion there).

Georges Prêtre, that exciting musician, conducted a weighty and fizzed-up account of the Overture, which made it sound as if it had been written by Beethoven. Then the curtain rose on the most beautiful and glorious production that, to this day, I have ever seen. It spanned a whole year: spring for the invocation to the goddess in the first act; high summer with a canopy in a forest for Adalgisa's admission of rivalry in love, and Pollione's humiliation, in the second; autumn for the aborted murder of the children and Norma's unhappiness in the third; and harsh winter with black bare trees against a leaden sky for the final tragedy and joint sacrifice of the last.

The tension in the house during the first scene of the opera, before Norma's entrance, was palpable. Would she appear at all? She did, surrounded by her priestesses, seemingly surrounded by a light or a nimbus (all charismatics have this in my experience). When Callas opened her mouth, would any sound at all come out? It did. The same voice that I knew from records, but smaller than I was expecting. *Casta Diva* was negotiated skilfully (a few notes omitted, a few runs simplified) and at her exit, she turned to the Druid army - and to us - and made an enormous, grand gesture of triumph.

It was clear to me that the secret of her stage art was complete relaxation, and that most of her effects were obtained with economy and often simplicity. Her body and her mind were a channel out of which came the music, the drama, the conflict. I remember every subtle gesture of her head, and the grace and wonder of the line and expression of her arms: relaxation and authority, that potent mixture which all great actors have. Although I have seen many actors and singers who compelled attention, there have been none, apart from

Callas, who not only made you keep your eyes on them, but who made you move and react with them, who made you even breathe with them. It is the only time I have ever seen Aristotle's catharsis in action, because I lived in the present through every moment that Norma lived, felt every emotion with her, and at the end, in her chosen death, I felt purged and exhilarated.

After I stood and screamed and shouted, and the Frenchman behind me said to his wife, '*Et nous croyons que les Anglais ne sont pas emotionnés!*' I forced my way past a surly *serviteur* to the stage box to shout *bravas* for her solo curtain calls. And Maria Callas (thank God she now had contact lenses) actually waved to me. My existence felt worthwhile and whole!

We were both too joyous and excited to sleep, and wandered around Paris in our evening clothes, sitting in a café as dawn broke. It was the first time I had stayed up all night. My mother and I were never so close again.

CODA

Seven years later I was twenty-one, living in Paris, doing some desultory work for a Mickey Mouse film company and auditioning for Jean-Daniel Cadinot (in his capacity as a maker of promotional films, I hasten to say, which he was then, rather than as the King of Quality Gay Porn, which he became). One night, I was picked up by a preppy young American, who had an apartment near the Arc de Triomphe. I left at about six o'clock the next morning, hungover and unshaven, and walked home to my room in the Rue Cambon. As I walked I became aware of a woman in my peripheral vision, beside me but a bit behind, who was walking two small dogs. I only saw her out of the corner of my eye but I knew at once that it was Callas.

'It's Callas. It's Callas. It's Callas!' I said, half-aloud to myself. I know she heard, because when we both stopped at the same time to cross a road, she looked at me as if she were trying to unravel something she saw in me. When the lights changed, I crossed, but she didn't for some reason. I turned again and again to look at her. She was looking at me too. I became self-conscious and hurried on, but felt compelled to turn again. She was still staring after me with eyes that had seen everything and understood everything.

CHAPTER THIRTEEN

DIABOLOS

During my first year at Bryanston, one of the older boys tried to kill himself. He lay down on a railway line, but when the train was almost upon him, he suddenly funked it, and tried to wriggle away. But it was too late, and both his legs were severed. He was found by workmen some hours later, bleeding heavily.

The press was naturally interested in a public schoolboy's gruesome failed suicide, and for a week the Crown Hotel at Blandford Forum was occupied by journalists hoping to scoop a tale of sinister deeds and bullying. The Headmaster, a smooth operator, told us to accept no bribes: 'Not even if you are offered five pounds.' It seemed that the matter was a solitary act of misery.

The day following the accident, a group of senior boys had gone to the railway and apparently picked up a few shards of bone and a piece of bloodstained sock. They brought these back to the school, where they were inspected by some, but not seen by me.

At Vaynol, after he had read the Court Circular in *The Daily Telegraph*, Michael read the *Daily Express*, and there he found the story. He wrote straight away to my mother in London, hoping that 'no other boy from the school was involved in this tragedy.' But he needed ammunition to justify his growing dislike of me, and was soon saying that I had been part of a gang who had tied this boy to the line (as in some silent Western) and that he had struggled free only at the last moment. He regaled visitors to Vaynol (especially ones who didn't know me) with the story of my 'attempt at murder' for the next two decades. I was twenty-six before I found out.

My father had a complete set of the plays of Oscar Wilde, inscribed by the author to Michael's grandmother, Lady Ripon. During a valuation of the house's contents by one of the major auction houses, they disappeared. It seemed obvious to my mother that one of the valuers must have been the culprit; but Michael thought he knew otherwise. My room was dismantled and searched. When the books were not found, Michael, undaunted, said I must have disposed of them for money. (How? I was only a teenager and did not know a single dealer.) The theft of the Oscar Wilde books was an accusation thereafter levelled at me - but only behind my back - until his dying day.

These were perhaps the ugliest of the many malicious fantasies he told against me, but he had many more for my mother, and some for others supposedly close to him.

He was *Diabolos*, in its ancient meaning of 'the Slanderer'. These slanders discredited me and did a great deal of damage. On discovering them, I thought his behaviour truly came from the devil. It was a behaviour I would hope not to see in anyone, let alone someone who stood in the place of a father.

As a last ditch attempt to salvage the family, my mother had persuaded my father that the three of us should go on a Swan Hellenic Cruise around the ancient sites of the Mediterranean. At the last moment, happily for me, he chucked, to go to Tangier and the boys instead.

On this cruise, my mother became lasting friends with Sir John Wolfenden, of the famous report which recommended that homosexuality between consenting adults in private should be legalised. Meanwhile I sat entranced by the classical scholar Sir Maurice Bowra, small, round and amusing, and Sir Mortimer Wheeler, tall, moustachioed and caddish. They talked across my head in the lounge, as I pointedly clutched Mary Renault's *The King Must Die* and E.V. Rieu's translation of *The Odyssey*. It was my first taste of academia, and I adored it. It was sad that I was so bad at my school studies and obviously not bound for Oxford, but I set my goal then and there on becoming an academic. It was one eventually reached, although by a long circuitous route. Sir Maurice seemed to take to me, and when I told him that I feared I would never make it to Wadham College, where he was Warden, he said, 'Never mind, Oxford is the coldest place on God's earth. Go to America!' When I said that I didn't think much of the approaching skyline of Beirut, he agreed: 'No. Skyscrapers and mud huts.'

* * *

My father adored being Lord Lieutenant of Caerna-fonshire, because he could wear a pretty uniform, fly flags on his car, and have judges bow to him. But he was not fond of the people for whom he was the Queen's representative. 'I wouldn't trust the Welsh as far as I could spit,' was an oft-repeated mantra.

Looking at photographs of Michael, I notice a change of appearance in the early 1960s. The wistful, amused face hardened, the mouth thinned and even began to disappear, his hair, now dyed jet-black, made his complexion seem florid, and his view of the world became increasingly distorted. He was a discontented man. He thought that the mistake that he had made in marrying Caroline had wrecked his life, and the fact that they had a child who was not even his compound-ed his resentment.

Meanwhile, for my mother in London, matters were hardly better. Audry's alcoholism (always topped up but never drunk) had caused early senility: 'wet brain'. Thereafter Audry would come first in her care and in her emotional energies. Sexual and romantic respite, both so important to her, were being found with the American artist, Marguerite McBey. They had met on a trip to Tangier to stay with her cousin, my godfather David Herbert. 'I have found my Waterloo,' she had apparently said to David.

She had also fallen out of love with me. As I reached adolescence, my manhood repelled her. No longer a dear little boy, I was becoming a problematic teenager, difficult to educate, over whom she had control no longer. Nor, any more, could she control the amount of love that I gave her. And this, since she was a woman used to having emotional power over others, angered her.

She also realised that I was gay. This appalled her. She thought it reflected badly on her, but also believed it would make my life unhappy. What horrified her seemed natural to me. All the interesting people I knew were homosexuals.

CHAPTER FOURTEEN

WHAT ABOUT THE LINEN?

The trustees of the Vaynol estate were becoming seriously worried about its vast expenditure. The quarries
were running at a huge loss and, in spite of very professional management, the estate was no longer supporting itself. Drastic steps had to be taken. One wing
of the house was demolished and (at vast expense) the
layout of the rest of the house was redesigned. The
kitchen gardens were abandoned to seed. The beautiful
lake was drained because the farm needed the water
supply, and a large hole was left in its place. In spite of
Michael's protestations, it did not look at all like a dell.

My hut in the woods remained, surrounded by an
ever-increasing tangle of undergrowth, because the
foresters had been laid off. I spent all the time I could
there, away from the house: dreaming, fantasising,
singing, reciting Shakespeare, and smoking. It was a
world divorced from obligation, where I was master,
and where I could find methods to transport me from
the mundane to the euphoric.

At Bryanston, I ran with the bad boys. (I have run
with the bad boys for most of my life, except now

most of us have turned our lives around and become good boys.) I combined rebelliousness with a pomposity that must have been extremely unpalatable. I wore make-up bought from Frizell's in Leicester Square: Leichner theatrical blending powder and mascara.

When the Headmaster summoned me to his study for one of my increasingly common delinquencies, I broke down and said my parents had separated. When my mother was asked about this, she had said no, this was completely untrue, and they lived together happily.

Bryanston had been chosen for its theatrical activity and I was allowed to act, usually pompous or flamboyant parts. The only close friend that I made during my time there was Michael Hucks, who also wanted to go into the theatre. He was a good boy then, and so he has remained.

I was in love with a younger boy whom, because he spent his holidays in the South of France, I shall call Marcel. There were romantic entanglements between our families: his mother had once been in love with mine, and his artist father had had a rather dramatic affair with mine, ending with Marcel's father jumping into a fountain in Rome in an unsuccessful attempt to drown himself.

I had a rival for Marcel's affections, a boy who later became the king of recorded classical music and *confrère* of Herbert von Karajan. I was vile to this poor chap who, like a cheerful Papageno, was much better-natured than I was.

* * *

I went to nearby Bulbridge for many Sundays. Simon Fleet would arrive at the school on Sunday morning, wearing jodhpurs with multi-coloured shirts, ginger wig aslant, heron-like legs folded into his mini, his pug-nosed, pop-eyed face exuding such benevolence. He caused hilarity among the boys and outrage among the masters, especially the sexually ambivalent Headmaster, who told my mother to ask him never to come again - a request that, to her credit, she ignored.

At those Sunday lunches, the regulars were Simon's boyfriend (and afterwards my dear friend), the artist Martin Newell, Richard Buckle, the ballet critic, who lived nearby at Bowerchalke, and assorted old theatricals: Noël Coward's bosom friend, the actress Joyce Carey, and the Lunts from America, avuncular Alfred and scary Lynn.

Then in 1965, Juliet, whose high blood pressure had not made her final years easy, died. Simon, in his mid-fifties, was allowed to stay on in the house for a year while her estate was being put to probate, to give him time to sort himself out. ('Why can't Simon get a job?' asked Aunt Veronica). Although in her final years he had complained vociferously about her demands, without Juliet, Simon lost his reason for being. He became adrift and it appeared that he was drinking too much, although in actuality his input was small but his head weak.

He continued to look after me on Sundays during the year that he lived on at Bulbridge. And sometimes Marcel came too. Long Crichel House, even nearer Bryanston, became the *rendezvous* for lunch. There, a quartet of eminent, civilized gay men lived together: the literary critic Raymond Mortimer, the music critic Desmond Shawe-Taylor, the painter Eardley Knollys, and the writer on music, Edward Sackville-West (who had recently become Lord Sackville, and was seldom there as he had decamped to his family seat of Knole in Kent).

Raymond I liked particularly, for his humanity and curiosity, not only about my life but also about my thoughts and feelings. Desmond took me to two London concerts, and after one, to dinner at the Art's Club, where I met the legendary music critic and cricket writer, Sir Neville Cardus. His music criticism is, for me, some of the finest ever written. As I listened to those two men discuss music, I realised that Desmond, who must have been in his late forties, was the baby, while Sir Neville was his respected grandfather.

After Simon's accidental death, one year after Juliet's, I continued to visit Long Crichel, bicycling over and listening to that informed talk about books, concerts, exhibitions, and artistic life in London. How lucky I was that those men allowed me to be there. They have my lasting love and gratitude. I learnt more in their company in three hours than I did during three years at Bryanston.

Simon died when I was seventeen, but his spirit has played a part in my life ever since, as it has for all who knew him. I wish I had his goodness and I wish I had his optimism.

One day in particular stands out for me. My parents and I were staying at Bulbridge for my June half-term. Leaving Granny to her afternoon rest, we drove over to Broadchalke, where Cecil Beaton lived. It was a day of early summer wonder, and the day Cecil writes about with self-aggrandizement in his diary (since published) - but I remember it differently.

Simon had given me a biography of the Empress Elisabeth of Austria, inscribed 'To Charley Hapsburg from Simon Wittelsbach', and I chattered about that on the journey over.

When we arrived, Cecil appeared with a splash of green paint on his crotch. 'What's that?' asked Simon.

'Paint,' replied Cecil.

'No, it's not,' continued Simon. 'I think it's spunk. Cecil is the first person to produce green spunk instead of the usual white.' (To a schoolboy this was beyond hilarious.)

'Simon, how many times must I tell you,' reprimanded my father, 'not to dot your 'i's and cross your 't's.'

Cecil's much younger American hunk of a boyfriend, Kin, was given a key to the cellar, and he and I went to fetch a bottle. On our return, we found Simon had gone to collect Dickie Buckle, and we all retreated to Cecil's Winter Garden, where Cecil then laid into my father about what provisions were being made for Simon after Juliet's death. According to Cecil, Michael said that he would receive some furniture, so Cecil told him that it was not furniture that Simon needed, but money. He was then informed that there would be no money, because Juliet survived on an allowance given to her by her son, but that Simon would inherit the house's upstairs contents. I apparently piped up with, 'What about the linen?'

Cecil's account continues:

> Michael, very cross, says, 'That of course comes to Vaynol.'
> Then I doggedly continue, 'But you mean Simon, after all these years, will get nothing?'
> 'Oh, of course I'll give him something,' says Michael, who is just as vague and intentionally mean as his mother.

Then, self-righteously, Cecil pronounces, 'It is sad to see that these selfish people get away without ever rewarding the devotion of the few who have made their life so much less difficult.'

Cecil was indeed told that there was no money left, but that everything in the house (apart from the Jacob chairs that already belonged to Michael) would, quite naturally, be Simon's. Even at fourteen, I cannot have thought that the sale of the linen would go very far. What I asked (more sensibly) was if there were other assets such as silver, jewellery, and linen that we could perhaps buy when Granny died, for Simon to have some immediate cash to tide him over.

Then the subject was dropped and we talked about Princess Marina until Dickie's arrival, when the conversation switched to Lilian Baylis of the Old Vic and Sadler's Wells, whose secretary was taking on some work for Cecil.

* * *

I rather used to like people to believe that I had been expelled from Bryanston, but actually this was not the case. After I had taken my O-Levels, it was plain that I couldn't wait to leave, and that the school couldn't wait to see the back of me. At sixteen, I felt ready to go straight into the theatre. My mother had other ideas, however. On her visits to Tangier to see Marguerite McBey, she had made friends with Joe McPhillips, an English teacher at the American school there. My godfather David and aunt Veronica Tennant already lived in Tangier, while my mother was beginning to visit regularly to see her new lover. The logical solution for my delinquencies was to get me there as well, and as soon as possible. I had met Joe, who had promised me the lead in the school play. I couldn't wait to leave England for the gay capital and drug centre of the world.

CHAPTER FIFTEEN

TANGIER 1966-7: CHILDHOOD LEFT BEHIND

Ellen Buckingham, in whose family I was to live for the next year, would be easy to recognize, my mother assured me, because she looked exactly like Dorothy Dickson - that star of pre-war musical comedy who stayed at Vaynol every summer, and who, in order to remain youthful, had blanked out her past.

The late-August Moroccan air, when I got off the plane, was like opening the door of an oven. It belonged to undiscovered Africa, not the familiar Riviera.

Ellen did indeed look like a bohemian expatriate Dottie Dickson: small, with mustard-coloured slacks, cork-soled sandals decorated with large red bows of her own making, many bangles, and a pretty but sun-leathered face. She was, I supposed, about sixty. With her was her daughter Desirée (Dizzy), only in her early twenties, dark, intense, with the Tangerine accent: home-counties English with the short American 'a' and an indefinable 'foreign' tune to it.

Ellen used to walk like a teenager, heels going clackety-clack, down the Tangerine streets, and the

Moroccan boys would follow her whistling, until she turned round and they retreated in horror. When, later, I was both the pursued and pursuer in such an activity, I privately thought of it as 'doing an Ellen'.

The Casitas del Farhar, where the Buckinghams lived on the Old Mountain, was a ramshackle collection of corrugated iron or cement huts, originally annexes of the Casa del Farhar, the large house further up the hill. Ellen and her husband Winthrop had for many years run it as a hotel/pension, and it had been the base for the early Tangier experiences of Truman Capote (who then drank only milk), Tennessee Williams, and Paul and Jane Bowles.

The Buckinghams, their family, and their friends delighted me from the start. The group drinking *sangria* on the terrace as we arrived were the local doctor, a retired solicitor, his wife, and the new clergyman of the English church where the Buckinghams worshipped regularly, as well as Dizzy's two little boys and their grandfather Win, a large, masculine, and benevolent *paterfamilias*. He, I grew to have the greatest liking and respect for. Although he was mocked by the fashionable queens of the New Mountain for his lack of small-talk, I sensed then and think still that those old Protestant American families have more integrity than any European.

The Buckinghams belonged to a respectable Tangier, a large and quite powerful expatriate community revolving around the British and American consulates, the Country Club, and St Andrew's Church, where my godfather David Herbert was church warden - one of the reasons for my residence in the town.

The Buckinghams were far less disapproving of the less respectable Tangier than most of their friends, because they were good tolerant Christians, and also rather amused by the shenanigans of the naughty. They were also less conventional than they appeared, for Win was really an American dropout, who had ended up on the North African coast after a bicycling tour of Spain in the 1920s. Ellen was a psychic and a witch.

Ellen was a missionary's daughter, born in Smyrna, whence her family were expelled along with all the Greek population when she was a child. She still spoke fluent Greek and read her Greek New Testament every morning. She had seldom set foot in her country, England. Her father had moved to Spain, where she met Win and his bicycle.

Ellen saw auras, read palms, and if the security of those she loved was threatened, she made wax figures, into which she stuck pins until the offenders, as she put it, 'left the country'. Her magic, white or black, only came from love.

Ellen placed books in my room, all of which I read for the first time: English classics like *Jane Eyre, Wuthering Heights* and *The Diary of a Nobody*, as well as *The Caine Mutiny*, Hermann Hesse's *Siddhartha*, and the works of Dietrich Bonhoeffer and Teilhard de Chardin. These alone would have made my year abroad worthwhile.

The Buckinghams liked swimming. This they did from the Windmill Bar, by far the nastiest of the many bars with changing-rooms attached which edged the town beach. They went there because the sea was warmer. It was warmer because the town sewer emptied at the end of the beach where the Windmill stood. One learnt to ignore the floating turds for the sake of a warm sea. The Windmill was owned by a slightly alcoholic gay couple called Mike and Bill. Win and Ellen seemed oblivious to the rather common English queens who were clearly having sex in the Windmill's lockless changing rooms with teenage Arabs, who touted their puny bodies on the beach.

One day the following May, there was a particularly obnoxious couple of Englishmen sitting in deckchairs, one good-looking, the other not.

'Christ!' the sexy one said, as whale-like Win and elderly Ellen in a frilly floral bikini came down the steps to the beach.

'And *he*,' said the plain one, looking in my direction, 'needs a cock up his arse.'

In my changing cubicle after the necessary shower, the door was first opened by a middle-aged attendant, who had tried that before and had it slammed in his face before. Then, to my heart-thumping astonishment, it was opened by the good-looking Englishman, clearly in a state of excitement. It was the first time I had sex with anyone other than a school friend.

Afterwards, Win and I sat in the car a while, awaiting Ellen.

'Sorry I'm late, darlings,' she said, getting in. 'I was talking to that charming good-looking young man. You probably know about him, Charley - he's a playwright. He has a play on in London now called *Loot*. He's called Joe Orton.'

'I've never had a hard-on over a middle-class kid yet,' Joe wrote in his diary two months later.

He had a short memory.

* * *

Living in the Kasbah, in a house with many doors facing onto a courtyard, was an artist in his seventies, whom I had known in North Wales. He was the director of the mock-Italian village Portmeirion. His house was called Dar Zero, and in the courtyard was the fig tree under which Samuel Pepys had written his Tangier diary. I only spent one full day with James Wylie and met him perhaps on ten occasions, yet he was one of the greatest - perhaps the most important - influence on my life.

Jim and his friend Ba Richmond-Brown looked like Ratty and Moley from *The Wind in the Willows*, in tweeds and homburgs, or battered straw hats in summer.

Early in my stay, Jim took this teenage son-of-friends for a drive and a picnic in the old cities of Chechaouen and Tetouan. He drove an incongruously trendy two-seater sports car for which, as he said, one needed a shoe-horn to get in and out.

It poured with rain all day, so there was no sightseeing and we ate our picnic in the car. But it meant that Jim could talk, and teach me (or in fact remind me of) something I had known forever.

On our drive south, as we passed a small walled town on our right, Jim told me a story.

'I was sent to Tangier when I was your age too, to learn Arabic for my entrance exam to the Foreign Office. One morning, two aides of the British Minister and I rode out as far as here, when we saw a Moroccan riding towards us. As he rode, I looked at that town, and suddenly there was a huge Union Jack flag floating above it, covering the entire sky. The rider told us to hurry straight back to the Legation, because the First World War had just been declared.'

Then he told me of his life as a psychic man and how he had, rather unwillingly, been drawn into the Spiritualist movement.

'At the end of that war, my brother returned home. He was perfectly charming but he was not my brother. He had been gravely wounded in France and his spirit had left his body, and another one had taken its place.'

'Or perhaps the trauma had just altered his personality?' I suggested.

'No,' said Jim.

Jim was what I later knew to be a 'seer': someone who has glimpses into the future. Such glimpses are often inconsequential or, as in Jim's case, unpleasant. He saw his mother, then a healthy woman, sitting immobile and speechless in a chair, which later came to pass, after a stroke. 'And I always know what people are saying about me behind my back, which isn't much fun in Tangier!'

'Here, you'd better read this.' He reached behind his seat and gave me a book called *The Boy Who Saw True*, the diary of a late-Victorian clairvoyant boy. It was a book that shaped my whole future, by reminding me of what I already knew.

'How did you guess I might be receptive to this?' I asked him later.

'I didn't guess. I knew when I first met you at Vaynol.'

I introduced Jim to Ellen, and they were able to discuss certain things which before they had kept to themselves.

'Don't try this by yourself. I think you're a bit unstable as yet for that.'

Naturally I took no notice, and was soon producing reams of automatic writing, which turned comically sinister: 'I am an evil spirit who has come to tell Charley how wonderful he is!' Such activity often produces gobbledy-gook, but it was a bit unnerving.

'Nothing I can do, dear,' said Jim, when I rather dramatically asked him to exorcise me. 'Write to the Spiritualist Association in Belgrave Square. They'll be able to help.'

I wrote and they replied with firm 'don't be so silly' advice, suggesting that I visit them when I was next in London. I did, and began my path, which started with psychic investigation and has ended in Christian mysticism.

'Be careful who you talk to about this,' said Jim at a later meeting. 'Most people will think you're bonkers.'

* * *

Also on the Old Mountain was a rather ugly modern house, built by the family who lived in it. They were a family with whom I fell collectively in love, and with the eldest daughter in particular.

Kathy Jelen was the daughter of the celebrated Hungarian polymath, Count Miklos Banffy: states-man, theatre-manager, and author of one of the great European novels of the twentieth century, the Transyl-vanian trilogy, which Kathy co-translated. In English it is called *The Writing on the Wall*.

Kathy was aristocratic in bearing, full of intelli-gence and humour, with charm like a tsunami and the loudest voice in the western world. I heard her long before I met her, screaming with rage or delight at her husband, children, or servants. She shared the school-run with Dizzy, Ellen's daughter.

Kathy did not enjoy this activity, and there was a lot of door-banging and engine-revving if there were a latecomer. Sitting in the back were her adorable youngest child David, then a boy of about twelve, and her two daughters: Lilibeth, the eldest, husky-voiced and voluble, and Nicolette, her younger sister, pretty and quiet. The Buckinghams' two grandsons, Georgie and Eric, sat in the front. All the boys went to the American school, the girls to the *lycée*. Lilibeth and I always managed to sit next to each other, legs pressed together. Later, emboldened, we held hands, a fact that did not escape Kathy, who was nothing if not sophisticated. She glanced at me sharply and silently in the mirror. I knew she liked me, and I her. Both of us were impatient and displaced.

In the chaos engulfing Mittel-Europa after the war, Kathy, after her family's Transylvanian estates were requisitioned by the communists, had married Ted Jelen, a Czech serving with the American army: a sweet, gentle, quiet giant. They had come to live in Tangier where Ted had a job with the Voice of America world service radio station. Here they built their house, and Kathy ruthlessly saved money to ensure that they had the standard of life, and her children the education, to which she thought their breeding entitled them.

Lilibeth had long sunflower-yellow hair, pale blue eyes, and golden skin, and I fell for her completely.

(Thirty years later, I was describing her to one of my students. She once arrived at a book launch in London with a large plaster on her nose, because she had just bumped it.

'I still think her the most beautiful woman imaginable. If she were a bit taller, she would be one of the great beauties of our age.'

'I think you're really heterosexual,' he rejoined. 'You just became gay to please your parents!')

She soon became of much more interest than automatic writing. We spent all of our spare time together, going for long walks - and I mean *long* walks. She liked the very early morning, coming into my hut at five-thirty and throwing a glass of cold water over my face. Like her mother, she was extreme.

Not understanding French education, ignorant of Descartes and Racine, I was amazed by the endless discussions of *l'âme* and *la philosophie*. Crammed with Conrad and Hemingway at the American school, I had a curter, snappier take on things. But I could recite a lot of Shakespeare, in whom she strove to find beauty, but I suspect found rather rough.

There was a lot of lying on the ground and heavy petting too. Nothing further, as she was quite rightly frightened of the consequences, although I remember her making me incredibly excited. She knew this, and my only intermittent sexual interest in women since has baffled her.

I returned to Tangier between my first and second years at drama school to see her. By then she had had an affair with a Moroccan poet who seemed to be cutting a swathe through both sexes in Tangier. She also had in residence a pretty young Frenchman called 'Petals' who later became her first husband. '*Mes bijoux, o mes bijoux*!' I remember him squeaking on the beach when he mislaid some trinkets.

I felt humiliated by her desertion, but she did persuade her generous parents to give the most wondrous party for me. They stayed away for the night, and it was a party to which all the youth of Tangier were bidden: Moroccan, French, American, English, all, of high and modest degree. Separate tables, Lilibeth on my right, wine and food beyond praise. It was a transforming party, a right-of-passage party. So many of those who attended have since sought me out and told me so. As we sat on the roof, watching the sun come up over the Straits of Gibraltar, drinking coffee and smoking kif, childhood was truly left behind.

CODA

A man and a woman in their middle fifties met in the restaurant at Waterloo station: Lilibeth in London to see her son, who was getting work experience in a bank, and myself. *Où sont les neiges d'antan?* indeed. She gave me a lighter in the shape of a heart - *un coeur en flamme* - not knowing that I had stopped smoking. After she left for Paris, a peaceful second marriage, and a good career as an interior decorator, I sent her a card with a picture that had meaning for me, and a letter which ended, 'What I have missed!'

CHAPTER SIXTEEN

I WILL NOT BE FLIP WHEN DISCUSSING EZRA POUND

Ellen, Jim, and Lilibeth gave me so much during my Tangerine year that my dismal failure at (and my dislike of) the American school has, in retrospect, bothered me little. However the negativity of that experience fed into my later life, for during that year I decided that, whatever work the professional theatre brought me, I would want to spend at least part of my life teaching. Watching Joseph McPhillips in action, I knew exactly the kind of teacher I did not want to be.

Joe McPhillips was twenty-nine at the time. He had promised my mother so much in London: intensive coaching for my English literature A-level, the lead in the school play, and the kind of older brother mentoring that Guy Nelder had given me at Frensham. But he made not the slightest effort to fulfil his side of the bargain. He gave me, I think, one session for a two-year A-level course, which it was deemed reasonable that I should master in three months. He had read none of the books or plays himself, and unsurprisingly, I failed. He had already decided that the school play should be a dramatisation (if that is the word for such a non-dramatic work) of *The Garden*, a Paul Bowles short story about a poor Moroccan who is persecuted for loving and tending his little garden. Naturally there was no part in it for me other than that of the narrator.

As he drove me home most days after school, I had to sit for hours and hours in Paul Bowles's spartan flat, silently and desperately praying that I would be relieved of the torture of hearing Joe and Paul waffling on about the inadequacies of faculty and students at some minor Californian college where Paul had taught creative writing. I silently begged God that I could soon go home and do my homework, all of which had to be written in capital letters, a trick Joe had learnt at the military academy he attended as a boy. Doubtless bullied at this place, he had become a bully himself, whose bluster was increased by huge amounts of alcohol. At Bowles's apartment, he drank bourbon while Paul primly sipped mint tea.

'Would Mr. Duff like some tea? Does Mr. Duff mind us talking so much?' asked Paul, which sounded odd coming from an eminent author and composer in his fifties, to a seventeen-year-old schoolboy. But at least it was respectful.

Joe also gave lines in true boot-camp style. 'I WILL NOT BE FLIP WHEN DISCUSSING EZRA POUND' five hundred times was one I remember.

Joe thought I was pompous and stuck-up, spoilt and gossipy, and he told me so. I was none of those things, just nervous. My natural enthusiasm for language and drama had been fragmented by his attrition of my confidence, and my imagination frozen by his constant denigration.

He saw teaching, it appeared to me, as an ego-trip and a power game. I realised that teaching had to be an act of generosity, whose three aims were to instil the student with a belief in their own abilities; to pass on the teacher's love of subject; and for the teacher to have engraved on his heart Plato's dictum that all knowledge is but remembrance. When I left drama school I swore an oath that no student under my aegis would ever leave my care without an added belief in him or herself. Because of Joe McPhillips, I was already well on my way to that conclusion by high school.

Joe's opinions were set. He had been taught at Princeton by teachers dazzled by Modernism. Sophocles was greater than Shakespeare and Pound greater than Eliot. Conrad was the greatest of novelists and you could not tell he was not writing in his own language (oh yes I could!). Dickens was dismissed as 'not serious'! Students were not qualified to hold contrary opinions or to think for themselves. Individuality - at least, my individuality - was to be suppressed.

Later, as Headmaster of the American school, he did good: bringing in Moroccans from poor families on scholarships, bludgeoning money out of people and institutions, convincing Yves Saint Laurent to help found a small American school in Marrakesh, and helping his students to further education the world over.

A few times in later years, tanked up with Dutch courage, he would call me in London to ask advice for a student wanting to train for the theatre. I was never of much help, although free with tips and goodwill. On such occasions he was almost shy and sheepish. He knew that I disliked him and he knew that I had cause. I also recognised him as a fellow alcoholic; he had that fatal mixture of grandiosity and lack of self-worth that so bedevils us. It is a tribute to him that sometimes his grandiosity was channelled into a largeness of vision that benefited his school, and maybe even Morocco as a whole.

I think Joe respected me for the fact that I took his treatment without complaint, and never talked about him until I was back in London. He also had to tread carefully with me, because he wanted to stay in the good graces both of my mother and my godfather David. He rather despised the superficiality of the *soi-disant* social elite, but he wanted their approval.

* * *

'Tangier,' wrote Cecil Beaton, 'is Cheltenham in the sun.' As always he had the *mot juste*. And a small town it was: parochial, self-regarding, hedonistic and sterile. Good French art-house films were shown in a small cinema (I first saw the Cocteau films there), but no decent theatre company came near the place; no orchestra and no gallery of any standard existed there. Culturally, Tangier was egregiously provincial, but its inhabitants were outraged if anyone suggested that this were the case.

These inhabitants were unbelievably self-congratulatory. They truly thought that they had recreated a society of glamour, style, and witty intelligent conversation not to be bettered in Paris, London or New York. In reality, nearly all of them were misfits who for whatever reasons (usually because they were homosexual) were not at home in their native lands. They were none the worse for that, and no doubt they flourished in ways they would not have done back home. But there was nothing special about them.

Tangier worked for you if you liked existing in groups, if you liked parties. Some of those parties were very splendid and exotic: fancy-dress in beautiful houses and hot gardens; drummers from the Atlas; musicians from Fez.

The *doyen* of this society was my godfather David, a Miss Mapp who had seen off his Lucia, a pretentious old bore and charlatan called David Edge. My godfather now reigned socially supreme, and alone.

David's sister, and my parents' cousin, was Patricia Hambleden, Lady-in-waiting to the Queen Mother. She was herself a great friend of David and my father, and many other camp men.

'I hope you don't mind me telling you this, Ma'am,' said David one day to Queen Elizabeth, 'but I'm called the Queen Mother of Tangier.'

'Not at all!' she replied. 'I wouldn't in the least mind being called the David Herbert of Clarence House!'

* * *

I had first come to Tangier with my mother (who had been before) for Easter in 1964, three years earlier. It was on this visit that Caroline had met Marguerite McBey.

We stayed with David (the 'Uncle Fishface' of my childhood, for he had protuberant eyes and sticking-out teeth) in his pink semi-detached house in the village of Jamaa el Mokra on the New Mountain. It had the most alarming entrance: cars had to negotiate a narrow driveway and get down a sudden steep incline. David had promised - loudly and often - to leave me this house, but that idea got lost when he fell in love, in his early sixties, with a Moroccan who treated him unkindly.

Living in the other half of the house was a terrible old termagant called Jessie Green who, having decided she was a 'character', felt free to be atrociously rude to all she encountered. Jessie had lived in Tangier since childhood, spoke the language to perfection, and loved the people. She terrified me, but my mother, a softer lesbian than she, knew just how to handle her.

David's small rooms were packed with good furniture, looking-glasses, pictures, and what my father called *bibelots*. They were all rescued from the Park

School, Wilton, where he had lived awkwardly on the estate of his parents, my mother's aunt Bee Pembroke and her philandering husband Uncle Reggie.

The sheets were damp and ants crawled around the lavatory seat of the only bathroom (which always smelt of gas), but I loved David's place and his life. I greatly took to his friends: Marguerite McBey, Janie Bowles (Paul's wife, at the start of the terrible illness instigated by a curse laid on her by Sherifa, her market-woman girlfriend), Candida Lycett Green (John Betjeman's daughter and our cousin) and her husband Rupert on their honeymoon, Adrianne Allen (Noël Coward's Planny-Annie and Daniel and Anna Massey's mother) and her husband, who were passing through. I loved my glimpses of *louche* Tangier, heady for a fourteen year old boy: the Parade bar, presided over by wrinkled Lily Wickman, who taught me to cook perfect scrambled eggs, and above all, the men, who lived together or who looked for other men in this liberal sexual climate.

David was huge fun too. A first-rate pencil-portrait-ist and decorator, he had channelled all his creativity into entertaining, counselling, and deciding who had *entrée* and who was excluded from his world, to which the socially ambitious of Tangier aspired.

He was often compared to his cousin, my father Michael, but he was a much less surreal character: his humour was earthier, and fuelled by a genuine and glorious high spirit and *joie-de-vivre* that Michael lacked. He was also by far the more intelligent of the two, and the wiser.

He was a delight to be around and to go on expeditions with, and our trip south to Fez that Easter was an enchantment. My mother took cine-film of David and me changing a wheel, after a puncture on a deserted road in the pouring rain. David's cow-pat hair, which he wound round and round his head to conceal his baldness, was streaming out behind him like pennant. Thankfully he later started wearing a wig.

David was a true wit. His flaw - and it was a marked and unattractive one - was that he was untrustworthy. He gossiped, repeated things he shouldn't have, and thereby made mischief.

David had gone to Tangier in the early fifties, after a piece of rough trade had tried to blackmail him as he stood in the queue at Martin's bank. He and his American lover Jamie Caffrey had taken up Jessie Green's offer to buy her house in Jamaa el Mokra, where they co-existed with difficulty.

Jamie, who had a drink problem and whom I liked enormously, departed for Spain where he became a successful designer of golf courses. David installed a surly Spanish manservant called Antonio, who had the bedroom next to David's, drove us around, and never spoke.

The other apex of Tangerine society was Aunt Veronica Tennant. She had moved from her beautiful but damp house at the top of the Old Mountain, where the orchids grew like weeds, to a bungalow at the bottom of it. The years of booze and cigarettes had caught up with her. She had become a gentle and defeated creature, with such severe emphysema that she was hardly able to breathe and was clearly not long for this world. I found her impossible to dislike, although my mother still managed to.

I had to fill in a form as a resident student, which needed to be signed by my next of kin. I wrote to my mother in London saying I imagined an aunt was closer than a cousin and godfather.

'No,' wrote back my mother, 'do not go near her. I don't want to be beholden to her for *anything*.'

So it was a slight complication, when Caroline took up with Marguerite McBey, that she and Veronica were close friends - and perhaps at an earlier stage, something more.

Both El Foolk, where Marguerite lived on the Old Mountain, and her house in Notting Hill - panelled rooms, pictures in heavy Victorian frames - carried the atmosphere of the Campden Hill school of artists of the early twentieth century. Marguerite's much older husband James had belonged to the world of Sickert and John. His huge studio in Holland Park Avenue, flooded with northern light from its immense window, had been kept as a shrine, and fascinating it was: convex mirrors which he had used as an artist in the First World War, stacks of canvas and brushes. To my eye his work is a bit dry and academic, although the etchings, watercolours of Arab scenes, and his portrait of Lawrence of Arabia are undoubtedly impressive. James, who died just before I met Marguerite, had rather kept her down, instilling in her a disbelief in her great gifts and originality. Her self-doubt remained, which I always found appealing.

After his death, she flourished. Having never dared paint while he was alive, she began for the first time, and I infinitely prefer her work to his: watercolours that are light, graceful, airy and atmospheric.

Marguerite always seemed the epitome of a style that owed its origins to nothing and no one else; an exoticism that belonged to no particular country or culture; a beauty which was wholly original.

With dark skin, shiny black hair up in a chignon, and exotic clothes that always suited her and never made a statement, sometimes she looked like an Aztec princess or a Pharaoh's consort, or sometimes just like an African village woman queuing at a well. She surely had black ancestry, although she swore she was wholly Jewish.

Miss Loeb from Philadelphia was her origin, and her great male love was the artist Oskar Kokoschka. She certainly changed Caroline's life and altered her view of herself and the world, which was liberating for both, since I think Caroline gave Marguerite a social confidence that previously she had lacked.

But in 1968, my mother was not yet secure in the relationship. I was sent away with a flea in my ear when I called unannounced at El Foolk with a grade sheet she needed to sign. 'Never do that again, ever,' came a note later in the day. And, in front of others, she unaccountably said to me (a very fastidious teenager), 'You haven't shaved, you haven't washed your hair, and I wouldn't be surprised if you smell!' Seemingly I continued to repel her.

Caroline and Marguerite travelled all over the world. For my mother, it was an essential escape from the horrors and sadness of Audry and Paultons Square.

* * *

I was beginning to sneak drinks from Ellen and Win's curious drinks cupboard: crème de cacao and the like. George, Dizzy's architect husband, found in me a drinking companion. He and I, under the pretext of buying something from the Socco Chico, used to sit in the dingiest and sleaziest bar in town, where George kindly (or otherwise) paid for all my drinks. We talked with the seriously alcoholic bar owner, who discussed at length the details of his appalling hangovers as he sipped Bloody Marys with a shaking hand.

Always sitting alone in this bar was the most revolting-looking elderly man I had ever seen. He had a plum-coloured but somehow grey-paste complexion, huge bald head, swollen nose, loose blubbery lips and pendulous jowls. His aura was one of decay and corruption. Sometimes he joined in our conversation, usually to make lubriciously salacious suggestions. His name was Gerald Hamilton.

Driving drunkenly home, George told me who he was: the original of Mr. Norris in Christopher Isherwood's *Mr. Norris Changes Trains*, whom *The People* had dubbed 'the wickedest man in Europe'. He had been accomplice of the occultist Aleister Crowley, conman, spy, and jewel thief, who had spent the war in prison for suspected high treason.

I last saw him in Tangier the day before the Prom party, the graduation ball, to which I took Lilibeth, dazzling in a white evening dress. (The opinion the other boys at the American school held of me was considerably upgraded.)

A few days later in Chelsea, as I walked along the King's Road, I saw coming towards me a homunculus among the beautiful people and Chelsea pensioners. It was Gerald Hamilton, and he leered at me as if he were expecting to see me.

'I saw you at the airport, but I hid at the back of the aeroplane and didn't address you.' (That can't be true, I thought, surely I would have seen him?) 'I didn't want to queer your pitch - heh! heh! - with your auntie Daisy, Lady Herbert. For some reason she's never approved of me!'

'I'm your neighbour now,' he continued. (How did he know where I lived?) 'I have a room above that emporium over there.' He pointed across the road to a Chinese restaurant called *The Good Earth* and bared unspeakable teeth. 'Better above the good earth than beneath it!'

CODA

In Tangier, through Marguerite, I had become friendly with Brion Gysin, artist and close friend of all the beat boys: Allen Ginsberg, Gregory Corso and Sinclair Beiles. He suggested strongly that I face away from the idea of R.A.D.A. and the West End theatre, neutralise my accent, go to New York, seek out Lee Strasberg and the Actors' Studio, and re-invent myself. I said I lacked the courage to do all that, so he said he would write to William Burroughs, author of *The Naked Lunch*, that homoerotic psychedelic trip. Burroughs was then living in London and Brion thought he would speak the same language as me: 'You'll be attuned to each other.' He gave me Bill Burroughs's number, which I was far too shy to call.

Then a Moroccan contemporary of mine came to stay at Paultons Square. He had known Bill well in Tangier, and he asked me to accompany him to Duke Street St James's, where he visited the man who was almost a god to the hippy generation.

Bill looked like the manager of a small town bank: grey suit, grey face, soft hat. I thought him one of the most sympathetic and wise old men (he was then in his late fifties) that I had ever met. There was no generation gap. He was somehow both our age and an elder statesman. He bought us some food in a pub in Duke Street, and I am still reminded of him every time I pass it. Afterwards we sat, one by one, in the

Perspex pyramid he had set up in his small sitting room, smoking joints.

This had a profound effect on me. I became very grave and silent, connecting to something deep within my spirit and psyche. Before we left, Bill said that he had noticed what had happened to me. 'It doesn't happen to many, you know. Please visit me again.'

'If he told you that, he means it,' said my companion as we had a long walk back to Chelsea. 'He doesn't say things he doesn't mean.'

But I couldn't believe that he really wanted to see me again, so I never called him. How very much I regret that.

CHAPTER SEVENTEEN

FAITH, HOPE AND CLARITY

Laurier Lister was an old associate of my mother's, with whom she had appeared in Barrie's *A Kiss For Cinderella* and St John Ervine's *People of Our Class* in the late 1930s. He lived with his partner of many years, the actor Max Adrian, at Shamley Green in Surrey. He had been director of the new Yvonne Arnaud Theatre in Guildford since 1964, and with his little moustache, never was a man so suited to running a theatre in the prosperous, unadventurous suburbs. (Surrey, as Nancy Mitford's Aunt Sadie reminds us, does not really count as 'country'.)

When I returned from Tangier in the summer of 1967, my mother, at a loss to know what to do with me, roped in our neighbour and the director of the two above-mentioned plays, Murray Macdonald. He suggested that Laurier might be persuaded to give me an apprenticeship.

Laurier, a kindly and unassuming man, offered me a cigarette from a large silver box and asked me two questions: was I strong enough to carry heavy weights about, and if I were put onstage, did I wear clothes well?

I said yes to both, and was scrutinised for a moment before he said, as if passing considered judgement, 'Yes, you look strong and you look as if you carry yourself well. Please start on Monday as a student Acting Assistant Stage Manager. We will pay you two pounds, ten shillings a week.'

The play was by J.M. Barrie again, *What Every Woman Knows*, and in the company were Dorothy Reynolds, who had written the book and lyrics for *Salad Days*, and her husband Angus Mackay. They were both as kind to me as they were, famously, to so many beginners in the theatre.

(The most important things in the theatre, said Dorothy Reynolds, are 'faith, hope, and clarity; but the greatest of these is clarity.')

I must have been the world's worst A.S.M. I had never fended for myself and had no idea how to tie up a parcel, let alone make a prop. However, as a buyer, I beat down shopkeepers and charmed local old ladies into lending pieces of Victorian furniture. I very much thought that with theatre people, I had found my tribe.

Laurier watched me during an understudy rehearsal of a dreadful play by a local author about the marriage of John and Effie Ruskin. He decided I had some talent and started to give me small parts. I knew that I had voice and presence, but little else. I was without technique, self-conscious, and obviously in need of training. It was a cause of resentment to some of the other young actors, who objected to working with an opinionated schoolboy. The hostility was slightly mollified by my obvious love for the theatre, about which I knew a lot, especially its history.

But outside the theatre, I was lonely, and beginning to escape into a safer world provided by alcohol. At Paultons Square, Audry was now in the most difficult early stages of her senility, still drinking quantities and burning holes in chairs with her cigarettes. So my mother drew down an invisible portcullis, forbidding me to enter the house. She rationalised this by claiming that I needed to learn to stand on my own two feet. But most of the other actors travelled from nearby London, and in my digs in Guildford, I was not only lonely, but often at a complete loss.

As the year spent in Guildford progressed, my usefulness to Laurier's little company diminished, and I was becoming a worry and a liability. Laurier saw me in his office, and said he wanted to talk to me 'like an uncle'. He told me, quite correctly, that I needed to go into a repertory company or to drama school in order to learn some basic craft and some discipline, because 'your talent is certainly worth it.'

Some found Laurier rather unctuous. He rubbed his hands like Uriah Heep and wore fake leather driving gloves. Moyra Fraser's father christened him 'Creepin' Jesus'. But I think of him with great affection. He stuck with me for a year because he felt some responsibility for my welfare and progress, and also because he saw something in me. I doubt many young actors would find such pastoral care today.

Max Adrian, Laurier's partner, was much more fun. He was a Dutch-Jewish-Irishman, a coruscating combination. His real surname was 'Bor' which was a great misnomer, as a bore he certainly was not. As an actor, he had an incisive individuality and a sparkling clarity. The measure of that talent can still be heard from his performance as Dr. Pangloss in the original cast recording of Leonard Bernstein's *Candide*.

I came to know him quite well on late-night train journeys from Waterloo to Guildford. He was playing Delius in Ken Russell's film about the composer. I was rehearsing *The Boy Friend* in London and travelling back to Guildford at night. In spite of his first class ticket, Max would sit with me in second class, where we would both talk loudly. Max was a 'card': full of gossip and good sense about the theatre. Michael Redgrave was Max's *bête noire*, since Redgrave had tried to black Laurier's appointment to the Guildford directorship. 'He sent me flowers when I was in hospital, and I sent a note back saying that I couldn't accept them but had given them to the nuns.' As he got into his chauffeured car at the station, he once said, 'Oh Lord, I do hope Laurier's made up the hot-water bottles!'

My father came to Guildford once. The play was N.C. Hunter's penultimate effort, *The Adventures of Tom Random*, in which I played a non-speaking character called 'Second Hostile Native'. Owing to confusion by the elderly box office manager, he sat in the back row of the circle and was under the impression that I was John Fraser, who played the title role. My very brief appearance passed him by altogether. His belief that I had asked him to Guildford under false pretences, and that I had never asked him to see me act anywhere else, was added to the catalogue of my offences.

On that visit, he was accompanied by a young lover whose presence in my father's circle made the lives of my mother and myself much more bearable. Edward Mace wrote the *Pendennis* gossip column in *The Observer*. He was the only person to be a friend to the three of us: my father, my mother and myself. In the earlier days of their relationship, he championed me to Michael, and I dread to think what my teenage years might have been without him. Edward was the voice of liberal, civilised London. His world, so removed from the fripperies of Vaynol, was a world of John and Penelope Mortimer, C.P. Snow, John Antrobus, Kenneth Tynan, and George Melly. Edward, one of the finest conversationalists I have ever heard, exhorted me to think about social concerns, revere ethics, especially as revealed through the arts, and laugh at pomposity and pretension.

Edward had another admirer, and one that I was anxious to meet: the director and producer Frith Banbury. Frith, bald, with a dog's-bum little mouth and hooded seductive eyes, lived in great splendour ('in more of a style than Sir John Gielgud' said one actress) in a house in St James's Terrace, overlooking Regent's Park. There he was looked after by a long-suffering Italian couple who lived in sub-human conditions in the basement. Frith, who was rather a snob, wanted to be asked to Vaynol, and my father wished to be kept abreast about the doings of stars of the past, so the pleasure of Frith's arrival in our lives was the one bond between my father and myself. (My mother, who had known Frith at the Players' Theatre during the war, always thought him and his work rather tasteless.)

A decade later, Frith and I became friends in our own right. He alternately delighted and infuriated me, and he was one of the three most influential shapers of my mind and character. A decade after that, I was to write a book built around his work in the theatre. But as a teenager, it was just gloriously glamorous to know him. From St James's Terrace, productions were mounted, plans were made, and famous actors were approached. It was a world of Binkie Beaumont, the Dames Edith and Sybil, Coral Browne, and best of all, my future dear friend, Robert Flemyng. It is a theatre now long gone, but one that, in spirit, I have never left - even if it has sometimes sat uneasily beside my less romantic and his-torically-based adoration of Shakespeare.

Edward also dragged Frith to see plays at my drama school, the Bristol Old Vic, where I trained after leaving Guildford in 1968. The class I belonged to at this school suffered somewhat by following a much more illustrious year, containing the likes of Jeremy Irons, Simon Cadell and Tim Pigott-Smith. The Principal, a chain-smoking old ex-communist called Nat Brenner, dismissed our year as 'the year the apple tree died' (an apple tree in his garden had apparently ended its life during our time). He seemed not to see students as individuals but as conglomerates: 'my light comedy year' or 'my Ibsen year'. When I came to run a drama school myself, I saw how idiotic such thinking was.

The same strictures could also be levelled at the revered and much-imitated movement teacher, Rudi Shelly, but I later came to know, like and appreciate him. Rudi, a Jewish refugee from the Nazis, saw his charges as artistic problems rather than as people with souls, and in my experience, ignoring a student's uniqueness as a human is a fatal error.

Nat Brenner was another male authority figure for me to set myself up in opposition to, but I did rather admire the old Leftie. He taught me to revere George Bernard Shaw as a thinker as well as a playwright, and he taught all of us how to act Shaw, whose polemic helped shape my burgeoning political conscience. (I was then unaware that Charlotte, Mrs. George Bernard Shaw, was my relation.) Perhaps Nat was cannier than I thought. Later he was to tell me that he thought my difficulty as a young man stemmed from the fact that I was surrounded by the wrong people.

I gained a lot from the singing teacher, John Oxley, and immeasurably from the old-school deaf voice teacher, Kathleen Stafford. She gave up her every lunch hour to work with a few of us individually. Katie was an elderly middle-class lady, of a kind to be found teaching in nearly every drama school up until the 1980s. She lived with her sister in a village near Bristol, and there she ran the local amateur theatre in the village hall, to which we were sometimes summoned to give poetry recitals. Long ago, she had been an assistant to the great voice teacher Clifford Turner, and she had stories of Robert Helpmann throwing tantrums as they tried to turn him from a dancer into an actor. Apparently it had been impossible to teach Vivien Leigh. Her methods may have been old-fashioned, but it can never be said of any of her pupils that we can't be heard.

Adrian Cairns, the Vice-Principal, was a dear, good man, a Quaker. He was not an imaginative director, nor, perhaps, an inspired teacher, but in his productions, I relaxed, my imagination unfroze, I lost self-consciousness, surrendered to the character, and enjoyed myself.

I am a great believer in the efficacy of drama training for all. Everybody should be encouraged to train as an actor, because you live as an equal to those of different backgrounds, whose families have other values to yours, and social effectiveness flourishes because shyness is brought under control. Best of all, you think great thoughts, speak glorious words, and develop, through Shakespeare or Chekhov, a knowledge of the human heart.

The great legacy of my time as a student was a friendship. Gerald Jones's father had been a South Welsh miner who had taken his wife and son to the better life of a foreman at the car factory at Luton. He had died when Gerry was teenager. As a drama student, Gerry was small, pretty, and not as Welsh as he wanted

(Luton had done its bit). He had the kind of face lucky for an actor: bright, which caught the light wherever he stood on stage. Obviously his world and experience were different to mine, and it seemed to me that his life had a substance and a strength that mine lacked. His education at the good grammar school in Luton was (looking at his schoolwork) a great deal superior and more stringent than mine at a public school.

Under the name Jeremy Blake, he worked with me again, but it is his family that has contributed so much to my life. He married young, and his wife Barbara has been the most wonderful, resolute, and steadying wife to him, and a loyal friend to his friends. They, and their daughters Emma and Rachel, were for many years my surrogate family and almost the centre of my existence. Rachel is my goddaughter, and seeing her grow up as closely as I did gave me a joy which is not the lot of many single men. My life would have been much the poorer without it.

* * *

In June 1969, while I was a student at Bristol, the greatest event of my father's life took place. This was the Investiture of the Prince of Wales at Caernarfon Castle. As Lord Lieutenant of Caernarfonshire, he was responsible for the arrangements, along with Earl Marshal, the Duke of Norfolk. He worked hard, and the success of the ceremony was largely due to his own effort. It was a great achievement. Prince Charles stayed a few times at Vaynol while I was in Bristol, and Michael's liking and respect for him was unreserved, as mine has been.

My mother also played her part, and played it well and with flair. She suggested that I take off the last week of my summer term to be there for the great event, just as she had missed a performance of Dodie Smith's *Call It a Day* to attend George VI's Coronation Ball in 1937. As I was in an end-of-term production of Chekhov's *The Seagull*, I naturally said I couldn't. I wanted to be an actor, not a courtier, and had I done so the school would have, quite rightly, asked me to leave. There was no conflict at all in my mind. However, I did enjoy watching the occasion on black and white television, and pointing out snobbishly but proudly that my Uncle Henry was carrying the Sword of State. Never, not for a moment, have I ever believed that Michael wanted me to be there. Nonetheless my absence was later used as another brick to destroy my reputation.

Fourteen members of the Royal Family had breakfast at Vaynol on the morning of the Investiture, the first time so many had been under a private roof. No Drino dressed up as Queen Alexandra, my father as Queen Mary, Hugh Cruddas as The Queen Mum and David Herbert as Princess Marina this time. It was the real thing and yes, it would have been a great experience to have been there. (Tony Snowdon, however, as Constable of Caernarfon Castle, was dressed up to look like 'the footman of some English queen living in Italy', as Liz von Hofmannsthal observed.)

Many were slightly shocked that my father received no decoration for his work on the Investiture. He had apparently said to Bernard Norfolk, 'I suppose I'll get the Garter for this.'

The lugubrious Duke had replied, 'If you go on dyeing your hair like that you won't get anything!' And he didn't.

***

At Bristol, others went home for weekends, but not me. Paultons Square was out of bounds. By now Audry needed nursing by professionals, and the sitting room downstairs had been turned into a sickroom. It was all far too expensive for Caroline, and her modest capital evaporated, but she was adamant that Audry was not to be put into a home. To deal with the emotional strain, she absented herself for long periods, staying with Marguerite in Tangier. After the Investiture, she hardly ever went to Vaynol again.

During the holidays, I stayed at More House in Chelsea, a rackety Bohemian boarding house run by a Roman Catholic gentleman called Felix Hope-Nicholson and his mother. It was the only private house in London with its own chapel, complete with a saint's relics and the hair of James II. The Hopes, who were fervent Jacobites and thought the Duke of Bavaria was the rightful king, had lived in the house for generations. They had known their neighbours Oscar and Constance Wilde well and I was shown a letter from a grandfather saying how dull and lacking in conversation Constance was. Felix sat on a window seat all day, in pyjamas and dressing gown, reading *Burke's Peerage*. He was a generous man, asking me often to dinners in a basement kitchen, cavernous like Baron Stonybroke's in *Cinderella*, with many hanging copper pots.

I lived in a tiny maid's room on the top floor, and my neighbour was the notorious Nazi spy Anna Wolkoff, who made a living as a seamstress. As her family had been forced to flee Russia by the Bolsheviks, she had sworn vengeance on all Communists and decided that supporting Hitler in her own small way was the best means to achieve this. It was she who had rallied support in Berlin for William Joyce's 'Lord Haw-Haw' broadcasts. She had spent the war imprisoned and was extremely lucky not to have been executed. She also had a particular hatred for my uncle Raimund von Hofmannsthal, who, as a Jew, had once, naturally, refused to be in the same room as her. She thought this a gross affront. Anna liked me, however, and said that she saw me as Romeo (nobody else did). She warned me against becoming like her friend Trevor Howard - in other words, a drunk. I once brought back a boy I had met in the King's Road. She heard us having sex and then, after we had drunk half a bottle of whisky, caught him puking on the stairs. 'It's a disgrace! It's a disgrace!' she wailed.

Even further upstairs, in an even smaller attic room, lived Anna's great friend Zena Douglas, the illegitimate daughter of Lord Douglas of Kirtleside, of Air Force fame. Once a famous good-time girl and drug fiend, she now stayed in bed all day, living on biscuits and the heroin that a doctor injected into her every afternoon. One night, her window was blown out in a storm. I was summoned to remedy this, showing that she had a very optimistic view of my abilities as a handyman. The sight of Zena sitting up in bed, her huge face framed by lank unwashed hair, white and horrified, has stayed with me forever.

* * *

Later, I spent the holidays in my great-aunt Diana Cooper's house in Warwick Avenue, where my cousin Louisa Farrell also had a room. It was then that I got to know this intelligent, egocentric woman, whom I had first met and feared in the music room at Vaynol years before, and who believed rules were for other people. Now she stayed in bed all day, lying in pink nylon sheets ('but they never need ironing'), looking like Dante with a bed cap tied under her chin, telephoning, writing, and receiving friends.

Diana was justifiably terrified of burglary after an unpleasant experience when she and Iris Tree had been tied up and robbed. I once disgraced myself by getting drunk and leaving all the downstairs French windows open all night. But Diana was quick to forgive. She was the most human of all my family. When I left, she hugged me (she disliked physical contact but said she liked kissing me) and asked, 'Have I been very difficult?'

'No, I've been difficult!'

'Yes, we're both difficult, aren't we?' she said with a big grin.

Of Diana's friends, I liked Iris Tree most; the poet, the hippy-before-there-were hippies, the wanderer, the spellbinder. I was so lucky to know her. I could ask her about her father Sir Herbert, the actor-manager: how he had played Richard II ('Christ-like'); how he had made the *Macbeth* film in very early Hollywood; or her own work with Michael Chekhov, Anton's nephew, and one of the great acting teachers of the twentieth century. She had played Lady Macbeth for him and in his community of actors and artists she had been a shining light.

The kindest of all Diana's friends was Evangeline Bruce, the wife of the enormously popular American Ambassador; the most unpleasant was Martha Gellhorn, last seen in Zell-am-See, as aggressive, unsmiling and rude as before. She had an obsessive emotional attachment to Diana and was almost insanely possessive of her. She hated anybody else being present when she visited. She was always openly hostile towards me and in her I sensed something frighteningly self-interested, cruel and heartless.

Diana liked my rent being paid in drink. My mother came round to do this, with bags of vodka and

CHARLEY'S WOODS

grapefruit juice, when Diana was out. Once she came up to my room and lay on the single bed as I sat in the only chair, and she said, 'Is there anything that you would like to ask me? Anything?'

'Like what?'

'You know. Anything.'

'Is there something I don't know that you think I ought to know?'

'Perhaps.'

'I'm at a disadvantage. You think I know something that I don't.'

'Do I?'

'Why don't you tell me?'

'You're going to hear a lot of things. A lot.'

'Like what, then?'

'You'll hear in time.'

'Then you won't tell me.'

'I wish you could think of some questions to ask.'

'Alright. Were people surprised when you married Daddy?'

'Yes, I think they were.'

'Why did you? Security?'

'Partly.'

'Did Daddy want to adopt a baby?'

'Shall we say, he did it for my sake.'

And there the conversation, started out with such honest intentions, rested.

CHAPTER EIGHTEEN

FROM PARIS TO LLANDUDNO

Edward Mace, the only friend of all the family, persuaded Michael, who persuaded the Vaynol Estate, to buy me a small flat in Bayswater. I felt myself to be very fortunate.

I had also met an English actor: a recently discharged bankrupt, beautifully dressed, ferociously heterosexual, and a compulsive gambler. A handsome man in his late fifties, he was called Neville Clarke. He lived in Paris and - under the name Tom Clark - was the resident English Gentleman in French films. 'If ever you are stuck over here,' he said to me, 'come over to Paris and I'll introduce you to my agent.'

I was stuck, and to Paris I ran, later selling the Bayswater flat to fund my rather extravagant life there. 'He sold the flat I bought him so he could drink,' said my father. In fact, I sold the flat so that I could get away and stay away from him or anybody else telling me what to do, and so I could leave London and the life of an out-of-work actor with increasingly decadent tastes.

The Hotel Cambon, where Neville found me another attic room, faced a side door of the Ritz. Rather shabby and sparse, it housed guests who could not afford the grander hotel but wanted to be seen leaving its Place Vendôme door. It housed also a strange trio of permanent residents, who consisted of Iya, Lady Abdy, Serge Lifar, and me.

Iya Abdy was a very tall Russian lady in her early seventies, with a mane of ash blonde hair and large hats. Her father George de Gay had been an actor and playwright of note in Czarist St Petersburg, and the family, in its early days of exile after the Revolution, had been supported by Rasputin's nemesis, Prince Yussupov. Iya spoke about Felix with affection tempered with acerbity, as she did about Diaghilev, Chaliapin, Stravinsky and the other Russian Parisians. We went together to Ken Russell's Tchaikovsky film *The Music Lovers*, which she found hilariously English (her marriage to Sir Robert Abdy had not been of long duration). We also saw Visconti's *Death in Venice*, which like me she found boring: 'That awful Russian woman singing at the end!'

Like Diana Cooper, Iya owned a chihuahua, except hers was black and had the longest canine tongue ever seen. 'No doubt it has its purposes,' said Neville Clarke, rudely.

Iya thought my life in Paris a disaster and urged me constantly to 'go back to your mother' - advice that, had it been taken, would not have earned her Caroline's gratitude.

In his memoirs, written earlier, Serge Lifar remembered Iya at the centre of the riot at the premiere of

Seconde Présentation designed by Miró, with a curtain of commas and smudges, and dancers in overalls. One of the Surrealists or Communists who disrupted the performance had his face slapped by Iya, who got her dress torn in return.

Lifar, the most handsome of Diaghilev's *premier danseur* boyfriends, looked, in his seventies, like a small, conceited black beetle. He tripped rather than walked, with head held high and a haughty stare given to any who met his eye. Many young journalists sought him out at the Cambon not (to his displeasure) to interview him about his great career, but to ask him about Nijinsky, whose trajectory from brilliance to madness had an allure that Lifar's life never possessed. I used to hear his exasperated tones, '*Non! Non! Non! Pour premier Nijinsky, et puis Lifar, et puis Lifar et après Lifar, et après ça Massine et les autres.*'

Lifar, like Lady Abdy, was a friend of the proprietor of the Cambon, M. Poisson, who claimed to be a descendant of Madame de Pompadour. The three of them had remained in German-occupied Paris throughout the war and had covertly worked for the allies. (Yes, Lifar too.) I imagine that neither of them paid the rent which, judging by their clothes, they could ill afford.

On most days, Neville would collect me from the Cambon and, after a few glasses of beer we would call on our bad-tempered agent M. Béars (known as Bare-arse) at his office in the Champs-Élysées. He found work for Neville, but hardly ever any for me. Then we would drop in on Ugly Agency nearby, who provided Neville with modelling work, but who refused to take me on because I wasn't ugly enough (or so I hoped). Then out to Billancourt (the French Pinewood) in the Bois de Boulogne and the studios there, to lobby casting directors for parts in films. Neville, with his flowing white locks and hooked-nosed patrician features, was in great demand. Then more drinks in the bar at Billancourt, with Neville spending my money buying whisky for old friends of his like Charles Bronson, or hoped-for new ones like Michael Winner.

Although he was a thin man, Neville was my Falstaff. There was too much alcohol and chaos around him for him to be exactly a life enhancer, but he dealt with life's vicissitudes with great aplomb and a lightness of touch that charmed all and delighted me. He was a gambler who was often being chased for money, and a womaniser who, even at sixty, had a bevy of widows and divorcees fighting over him. He was reprobate and a lush, but he showed such gaiety in the face of adversity and such absolute tolerance of the foibles of the world, that being in his company was somehow safe. One felt secure; whatever happened could be coped with.

He took me to my only heterosexual orgy in a house in the Ville d'Avray. For some reason I was required to put on a suit and tie to arrive at this establishment, although these were soon discarded. There were lots of middle-aged, middle-class ladies and gentlemen fucking each other, with a few young girls (house-girls, I presumed) adding some eye-candy. A thirty-some-thing businesswoman pursued me, and I suppose she got what she wanted, for when I awoke the following morning, my hands and other things smelt very fishy.

Neville had a small film distribution company called Ashley Films, which slid in and out of insolvency. This company had acquired the script of a thriller called *The Illusionists*, and very clever it was, with aston-ishing twists and sleights of hand. We were meant to promote this property in Paris and a lot of my money was spent giving free-loading film people dinners. But, in spite of angry letters from Lloyds Bank in Port Dinorwic, it was great fun and such an experience. Like all young men, like Prince Hal, I needed to go through the tavern in order to reject the tavern. Paris was my tavern and Neville was my 'latter spring, my All-hallown summer'.

* * *

I knew that I was meant to be in England trying to be an actor, where friends and contemporaries were establishing themselves. (Gerald Jones, now Jeremy Blake, was at the Citizens' Theatre in Glasgow.) But I was drinking in order to mask a real feeling of failure to achieve, and alcohol was beginning to get the better of me. The jobs, when they came, were not distinguished. In 1976 I landed up at the Grand Theatre in Llandudno for a summer season. It was not exactly clever to place myself half an hour's drive from Vaynol and my father.

Not indeed that Michael ever came to see me, but twice he sent over spies, young men who were his hangers-on and who had never met me. These men, some of whom were loosely connected to the theatre, sat in the front row, talked during the performance and booed me at the curtain call. I know who the ringleader was and I have not forgotten.

The Grand was an Edwardian theatre in a sorry state of disrepair. Its owner was an eccentric recluse called John Creese-Parsons, who lived in the mountains and who never, not once for the whole season, visited the theatre. On the programmes he was billed as 'director', and when anybody questioned this attribution he said, 'I direct by telephone.' Even if this practice had been possible, his assertion was untrue. After meeting him in his mountain retreat before the season started, he never addressed a word to me again, not even after the season ended when the actors sued him for unpaid holiday money, in a case where our most able union representative was Kenneth Williams.

We rehearsed the plays: *The Sound of Murder, Dial M for Murder,* and an American comedy so terrible that its name is mercifully forgotten. I only remember the performances because I, playing a Bobby Kennedy-type senator, had to cross the stage, lean over the back of a chair, and kiss another senator's wife, played by Diana Bradbury, on the neck. The buckle of my belt caught her lovely red wig and pulled it off, so a large red sporran swung from my waist and Diana sat in the chair with a bald cap on. It got the biggest laugh of the season.

The youngest member of the company was Reggie Oliver, since a distinguished dramatist and biographer and writer of the best creepy short stories in the English language. One, *Beside the Shrill Sea*, owes a lot to that season in Llandudno: he describes the company as 'no more than averagely competent'. This, I felt, was an overly kind assessment.

John Creese-Parsons's much younger wife Laura, a little mousey thing, ran the box office and disappeared to the mountains after the Saturday night show to present our director with the week's takings, and to cut his toe-nails.

I took Diana Bradbury, who was slightly older than I was, to spend each Sunday with my Aunt Rose McLaren at Old Bodnod nearby. Rose, now retired from Soho and the Colony Room and living the life of the respectable country lady, was the only member of the family to be kind to me when others weren't. She had unquestionably the finest character of all my mother's siblings.

Back in London, I moved in with Diana and her mother in Clarence Gate Gardens, Regent's Park. Mrs. Bradbury always reminded me of one of Jane Austen's stupider women, Mrs. Bennet or Aunt Norris. Diana was in love with me, and my lack of reciprocation pained her. But I did adore her energy and real ability to amuse. Her vividly individual talent as an actress was undermined by stage fright, which she unwisely camouflaged with alcohol. Her emotional life had been permanently scarred by a husband who had made her have five abortions in five years. The Bradburys looked after me and fed me when times were hard.

Escaping from Diana, I would visit Simon Fleet's boyfriend, Martin Newell. He was a sweet, attractive, but very alcoholic artist living in a studio in Sydney Close. Here we drank cheap red plonk or, when funds were exhausted, a disgusting mixture of meths and milk, which we called 'purple flashes'. We were lucky not to go blind.

James Pope-Hennessy, that great biographer and Aunt Bridget Paget's fling, came back into my life with his variety, education and erudition. His *Sins of the Fathers* is the best book on the slave trade, and one that I recommend to every American university I work at, where ideas of England's role in that trade can be inaccurate to put it mildly. He was and has remained my *beau idéal* of a man of letters. 'Tell me more about yourself, Charley Duff. Tell me more.' And he genuinely wanted to know. Three days before his death, I saw him at the *salon* of an old toad of a hostess called Viva King. Two young men had read, incorrectly, that he had received a large advance for his planned biography of Noël Coward. His death was manslaughter. His charming companion Leslie Smith was horribly injured trying to defend him. It was my melancholy duty to break the news to Aunt Bridget, and go to her flat and sit with her for that evening.

I was having a short affair with a professional pianist, who one evening took me to what was then called a 'queer party' in Orme Square. It was the smartest of any such party that I had attended. There I met a conventionally dressed man, older than myself, who seemed to have a most flattering interest in me. I had seen him before, because he was the proprietor of a trendy bistro in the King's Road called 'Nick's Diner'. Nicholas Eden was the son of the ex-Prime Minister Anthony, my mother's old lover. That much I knew. We sat together on a sofa and, as the evening wore on, snogged mildly. Later my pianist friend heard him say, 'I've just been kissing my brother!' Suddenly I realised what was meant. Could it be true? The possibility gave me a certain *frisson*. What if I had been lied to all these years and I really was my mother's son by the ex-Prime Minister? I thrust the whole matter deep inside for the time being.

I had a lot of sex in the seventies, some sober, most drunken, but no real love affairs. Then one summer's evening in 1975, during a period when I was on the wagon, I went alone to a performance of Tom Stoppard's *Travesties* at the Aldwych Theatre. Perhaps rejoicing that that gloriously funny comedy of language was back, I took my time and was one of the last members of the audience to leave the foyer. It was then that I saw a tall, good-looking young man, with dark curly hair and blue eyes behind spectacles, staring at me intently. A bolt of energy struck that both exhilarated and enervated me. It was as if I were in shock, and I turned and left the building hurriedly. I felt his look as I walked away, and everything in me urged me to turn back, start talking, and told me that if I did, the meeting would be ordained and beneficial. But, for some reason, I lacked the guts. When I met that young man again, six years later, I found out that he was a student who had a holiday job as the follow-spot operator that evening. After that there was a story.

CHAPTER NINETEEN

SACKED

Caroline was well aware of Michael's slanders against her, but she stayed admirably silent until one day, seeing a chance to off-load her past, she suddenly shafted him.

Michael needed cash for the estate. In 1975, in order for the trust to be broken and money released, the trustees needed to ensure that Michael never remarried and had more children. Signatures were required from both Michael and Caroline on a document stating that their marriage was blissful and constant and would be forever until death.

Caroline said yes, she would be happy to sign, on the condition that the estate paid her seventy thousand pounds. She wished to buy the leasehold of her house in Paultons Square, where Michael had never been invited to spend a single night. He was appalled. He telephoned Edward Mace at three o'clock in the morning and said, 'Come round *now* because I think I'm going to die.'

But the money was handed over and, once she received it, Caroline promptly put the house on the market. She summoned me to Paultons Square and we sat in the garden. I believed we were on good terms.

'Aunt Diana tells me that Martha Gellhorn has sacked her son,' she began. This was the boy from the Italian orphanage whom I had fought with on the ski slopes, and over whose adoption my mother and Martha had quarrelled vigorously at *Mosshammer's*.

'Is that so?' I replied, somehow knowing what was about to come.

'Yes, and she has suggested that I sack you. She said, "Why don't you sack Charley?"'

'Don't be silly. Diana often speaks before she thinks.'

'Not this time. I'm going to take her advice.'

I laughed. 'I don't think one can sack one's son.'

'Well, I think one can.'

Then for half an hour we talked quite casually of this and that, and then I got up to go.

'Goodbye,' she said.

'Goodbye.'

I felt quite calm, even serene. It was surreal. Although I spoke to her on the telephone when she was dying in hospital six months later, I never saw her again.

She went to stay with Marguerite in Tangier that autumn, having bought a small flat for herself and Audry in Maida Vale, to be near to her sister Liz. While in Morocco, she experienced severe stomach pains and returned to London for tests. These revealed incurable pancreatic cancer.

She booked herself into the London Clinic that November, and Michael thought only of the huge bill being accumulated. 'We shall be *ruined*!' he said to all.

She had satisfactory revenge on him, spinning out her life until the following March. Then he had to foot the entire bill for her illness and death. (Marguerite kindly paid for the extras - orange juice and the like!)

Many visited her, even Michael once (although she gave him only a letter for her executor Charles Farrell). However, her sisters Liz and Kitty kept me firmly away. I was hurt by this attitude, as I loved my godmother Liz and had always received such kindness and hospitality from Kitty, my youngest and most high-spirited aunt. I telephoned my mother once or twice but, although perfectly civil, if drowsy, she seemed to have let go of worldly attachments. I ceased to trouble her.

I had spoken to the matron at the hospital the previous evening, who had told me that the end was imminent, so I was not surprised when Liz rang the following morning to say it had come. I was slightly nonplussed, however, when my father telephoned that night.

'Caroline' - not 'your mother' - 'died half an hour ago,' he announced in high good humour. I knew that this was untrue.

'Yes, it's very sad that she has,' I ventured.

'And *awful* for us, of course,' he concluded cheerfully.

I minded, because there was still a side of her that I loved: feminine, vulnerable and unsure. Perhaps only I saw it, and seldom at that. She was sixty-two.

In her will, everything was left to Audry, who was put in an expensive home and died a year later. I received a quarter of the little that remained.

Her sisters emptied her flat.

Michael, Marguerite, and I met for dinner in Marguerite's house in Holland Park Avenue a few days after her death. It was truly awful. Both Michael and I got drunk and said terrible things to each other. It was the only real open row that we ever had. Marguerite sensibly made Michael leave the house while I was in the loo, and then she sat me down and talked very frankly. I don't quite know why she chose to do that, but I'm glad that she did. She told me that I needed to face the fact that my father had been against me for a very long time, since I was tiny. It might be due partly to jealousy, she didn't know, but her advice was that I should never try to see him again. Even through the screen of booze, I was taken aback and shaken. But I remembered.

CHAPTER TWENTY

DRINK AND DEATH
AND RESURRECTION

At Vaynol there was a storm, and a tree crashed into my hut in the woods - Charley's Woods - and shattered it. 'Lucky you weren't in it,' said Les Bowles, who helped clear up the wreckage. No chance of that, I thought, for I never went to Vaynol anymore - except once, for a short sober weekend, when Michael bizarrely insisted that I should bring a friend.

When the house was being expensively altered for the worse in the early 1960s, Michael had commissioned Simon Fleet's lover, Martin Newell, to paint a mural in the new marble-columned hall. Martin's *trompe l'oeil* extravaganza had scenes of romanticised North Welsh life: my father riding an elephant, my mother sitting on a stile, me standing at the top of the first Marquess of Anglesey's column.

On arrival, I proudly showed my friend my place in the mural - only to find that I wasn't there. I had been painted out with a splash of coarse dark green paint. It made it worse to think that it was my friend Martin's work that had been thus defaced.

Michael had surrounded himself with a new set of friends, youngish gay men on the fringes of the arts. Some I came to know later and to like, but not all.

At their centre was a schoolteacher from Chelsea with literary ambitions. His effect on my father was wholly deleterious. He fanned my father's resentments and encouraged his dislike, even hatred, of me. Much of the content of the poison-pen letters that I regularly received seemed to be words and sentiments that I sensed emanated from this man. I knew my father had to demonise me in order to justify his attitude.

'Michael was so stupid,' said Glur Dyson-Taylor. She was the ex-wife of Peter Quennell, a friend of Michael's, who later became a dear one of mine. 'For a man like that, having a son could have made such a difference to his life. He had a lovely boy like you, who, had he made the effort to love him, could have made him so happy. Both of you happy.'

I had, at his time, a short-lived boyfriend who purported to be the son of a Royal Duke. If this were true, he was as drunken and unpleasant as his father. Michael was pleased about the Royal connection, and asked this boy round to his flat in Cadogan Gardens behind my back. There he made a pass at him. When the boy protested that he was in love with me, my father said, 'He's not worth it. He's a harbinger of doom.' My friend then told my father many things that I had told him in confidence, and great harm was done.

My father also developed a crush on a man whom I had known in Paris, who told him about some of my escapades there that should have remained private. Great harm was done again.

The hatred between my father and myself was now of hideous proportions, and judging from the content of his angry letters, he was blaming me for the wreck of his life. I formed a fixed idea that one of us had to die before this malign state of affairs could be lifted.

It looked as if my black prayers were being answered, for a growth on my father's neck proved to be cancerous. The operations, combined with lengthy treatment to combat this malignancy, greatly weakened his health and depleted his spirit.

'Charley will never be alright until you die,' Edward Mace had told him.

'I know,' was the reply.

Shortly before his death he sent me a letter. It was not a poisonous one. Enclosed was a cheque for fifty pounds, and an expression that he was glad I was happy in my work (I would have been, had I had enough). It continued, 'There is a lot wrong with the world and there is nothing you or I can do about it.' That was, I knew, an oblique reference to us, and that letter was his best effort at goodbye.

Then, in 1980, Diana Bradbury took uncharacteristic action. She had the opportunity of moving to the country, which she wished to do, but she felt obliged to see me sorted out first. She arranged for me to be admitted to a National Health hospital in Epsom, and afterwards to a treatment centre on Kingston Hill. While I was being dried out at Epsom, she rang me to say that Michael had died of the throat cancer that he had been fighting for six years. For the last two I had not seen him.

I was in a dire physical and mental state when this news arrived: shivering and shaking with withdrawal from alcohol. But I knew that from then on everything would be alright, if I chose it to be. I missed the funeral at Vaynol but attended both of his memorial services, one at Bangor Cathedral, and the other at Chelsea Old Church. I felt calm and dignified at both, although at the latter the schoolteacher from Chelsea did his unsuccessful best to attack me.

Diabolos, the Slanderer, was dead. I was liberated.

While in treatment on Kingston Hill, I received a letter from the trustees of the Vaynol Estate. Enclosed was a document, which I was told to sign and return. It stated simply that I undertook to lay no claim on the Vaynol Estate, whatever the circumstances. Anxious to please and guilty for trouble caused, I signed. It shortly became clear why they were so anxious that I should. Just six months later, the law which stated that adopted children could only inherit what was specified in a will was altered. Adopted children gained the rights of natural ones where inheritance of property was concerned. Had my father lived for just a few months longer, I could have sued for everything he owned, rather than inheriting just five thousand pounds out of an estate worth nearly a million. But my self-esteem was so low I doubted that I merited anything.

I believe, after many years of recovery, that every alcoholic is on a spiritual search: 'seeking spirit through spirits'. However, it is a mistaken spiritual search, because the addict tries to fast-track that which can only be attained through the hard graft of a spiritual programme. This programme has to be based on taking the focus away from self, on the dissolution of the ego. We have to use our own experiences to help others similarly afflicted. Helping others is the antidote to self-centred fear, just as gratitude is the antidote to self-pity, and compassion for others can only come from self-forgiveness. In the end, all anger and hatred is self-directed. 'Who loves himself can never harm another,' said the Buddha.

My spiritual search was thereafter to turn to healthier and happier channels. I let in the light. I was helped by others who had been there before me. I was helped by love, the giving and receiving of love. I never felt hatred again.

CHAPTER TWENTY-ONE

RETURN TO VAYNOL

In 2005, B.B.C. Cymru made a documentary about my return to Vaynol after, it was believed, an absence of twenty-five years. (I had actually walked around the grounds, but not gone into the house, a few years earlier.) Locally, in Gwynedd, little was known about the Vaynol of my parents' time. What happened behind that grim seven-mile wall was something of a mystery. So the title chosen for the film was *Faenol; Secrets Behind the Wall*. However, like all mysteries, there were fewer secrets than the producer of the programme had hoped for.

So many rumours about my parentage had filtered through to me during my life that when the producer faced me with this new one, I was poleaxed. If truly, for fifty-five years, many in Gwynedd had believed me to be the illegitimate son of the nineteen-year-old Princess Margaret and Group-Captain Peter Townsend, I must have had an aura of glamour that I didn't know I possessed. I had earlier told the producer that I had white hair. As I alighted from the train, I could read the disappointment on her face and that of her assistant. Obviously they had hoped to see a little white-haired Princess Margaret-man scuttle down the platform, rather than the slightly overweight professor of six foot one who emerged.

I thought that the idea of the Queen's sister being able to have an illegitimate child then, or at any time, without someone talking, was so idiotic that I could hardly marshal arguments to disprove it convincingly. So this rumour is still to be found on the Internet.

The other mystery didn't concern me. I wasn't asked about it until my contribution to the thirty-minute film was over. Then it was talked about by a local historian on camera. Apparently, just before the Vaynol Estate was sold by Andrew Tennant, my father's heir, this historian had asked if there were any documents that he could peruse. The estate manager had shown him a room packed with documents (in fact the old squash court) and told him he could take the lot. It was a veritable treasure-trove, he said. When he returned the next day with a van to collect them, they had all been burnt. 'We couldn't have people seeing those.' It was privately assumed that there had been material concerning my father's sexuality. But I knew exactly what was in the squash court. Indeed, there were things of value - to me anyway - but nothing more scandalous than old estate accounts and, perhaps, the most mundane personal correspondence.

However, my books were there and I assume they were burnt. Years previously, my father had cleared out my room to give it, with my full (if unasked) approval, to our darling Dilys Hughes, the housemaid.

The glamorous books about theatre were transported downstairs, the rest moved to the huge pile of junk in the squash court. Among the books thrown out were a few tatty but autographed scores that had once belonged to Juliet: Puccini's *Madama Butterfly*, with the violin bow marks written in the same ink as the composer's own dedication, as well as inscribed scores by Massenet and Saint-Saens. These must have been burnt.

Presumably this bonfire of the vanities had taken place just in case there was anything incriminating about my father. How pleasing, that someone had had such a sense of family loyalty.

* * *

During the documentary, the viewers were informed that 'Charles Duff leads a life very different from the aristocratic one of his boyhood.'

In 2005, I had just had a long spell of teaching at America campuses on both sides of the Atlantic. I was a kind of 'Shakespeare Out of a Suitcase' proselytiser, speaking to schools for both rich and poor, and once, like a Shakespearean Billy Graham, to a stadium of two thousand.

Andy Tennant had dismantled the estate and sold off as much of it as he could, piecemeal. The central block of the house and the immediate surroundings, gardens, deer-park, and farm, were bought by an excellent local man. He has cared for them well and restored the lake, if not quite to its former glory. Meanwhile, his son has restored the manor house, so shamefully neglected by my family for three hundred years. This 'Old Hall' is now inhabited by his family and, being loved, has flared into life again.

Most of the proceeds from the sale went to Andy's daughter in Australia. I certainly received nothing, and indeed expected nothing. Andy invested, as an interest-free lifetime loan, the same modest sum into both the house of the estate manager, and into my small London flat. Clearly to him we were equated.

Vaynol – or rather the Welsh, *Faenol*, 'manor' - had become the venue for Bryn Terfel's August Bank Holiday Music Festival: one day of opera (with Carreras and Gheorghiu one year), the next Van Morrison, the next rock. As such it has become known throughout Wales, but not perhaps as much as it should be internationally. I have never been to it, although I was once asked. But I am so glad opera is being heard at Vaynol again, after me blasting the house apart with Callas and di Stefano. It contents me to think that so many are being given pleasure there by music, and by the setting of the lake and illuminated house.

In 2005, businessmen, estate agents, surveyors and the like had rented space for offices in the upstairs bedrooms. Downstairs, in the white-and-gold drawing room, you could hold your wedding reception or have a party. In the rest of the house, a body funded by the

Welsh Development Board was meant to be running a scheme to teach the delinquent young unemployed. While I was there this scheme seemed not to have a single student, but there were a number of smartly dressed young men in black, hanging about not doing very much. I kept seeing one of them looking at me from behind various trees, as I walked about.

Vaynol always had a smell all of its own. It was a smell I have found in no other house. I have no idea what the smell is of. It is not scent and it is certainly not mustiness. It suggests, perhaps, a certain luxury, comfort, and safeness. That smell is still there. When I asked someone who worked in the house whether he knew it, he said that he did and that it was unique, to be found nowhere else. I do hope it is indestructible.

The first time I came back to Vaynol was during Andrew Tennant's ownership, although while he was away. I felt my father's presence still. It had been his life for seventy years, after all. But by 2005 he was completely gone, I hope for his benefit as well as mine. I noted that there is now a 'Lady Caroline's Walk' and 'Charley's Woods' on the estate, but nothing called after Michael.

It was not my place in the family, but the house itself, that now seemed to speak to me. My life had been as important in its three-hundred-year history as anybody's who had lived there. No child could have loved it more, or have observed in it such strange goings-on.

The highlight of the documentary for me - and indeed for most of the viewers - was the contribution made by those people, now old, who had once worked on the estate. There was also an interview with Derek Randall, George the chauffeur's son, who had, like me, grown up there.

I hadn't seen Derek for some years. We were both now in our fifties, and I was so taken aback to see him suddenly looking like the image of his father. Moved to my very depths and speechless, I asked for half an hour's break to go for a walk and compose myself.

I wandered past the lake to the woods named after me. The hut was long gone, and only the stump of the tree that felled it remained. The day was beautiful. And, with their undergrowth of brambles and wild flowers, Charley's Woods were beautiful.

CHAPTER TWENTY-TWO

DUNMANWAY AGAIN: IN THE SHADOW OF THE GUNMAN

Here is the story of my real grandfather.

David Gray, born in 1884, was one of five brothers from County Cavan in the Province of Ulster. His parents, Robert and Mary, were Anglicans of perhaps English, perhaps Lowland-Scots descent. Their ancestors were settlers who, in the seventeenth century, had been given a farm, confiscated from Roman Catholic 'rebels'. Others of the minor Protestant Ascendancy, who had similar farms worth ten pounds a year in the Irish census of 1847, called themselves 'yeomen' or even 'gentlemen'. But the Grays were not armigerous, nor did they crave status, and they were content to call themselves farmers.

The five boys and their two sisters lived at Barnagrove, close to the Monaghan border. All the family were musical and all, except David, loved the outdoors.

Davy was bookish and clever. Somehow (perhaps by apprenticeship and correspondence course?) he qualified as a Licentiate of the Irish Pharmaceutical Society, and moved south to West Cork and the pretty market town of Dunmanway. There, according to the census of 1911, he was lodging with a family called Ashe and paying rent for a chemist's shop in Market Square, which he rather grandly called 'The Medical Hall'.

There was a sizeable Protestant minority in Dunmanway, most of whom lived in Sackville Street, hard-by the local Anglican Church. David soon became a Church Warden. When his business prospered he bought a house, and married a local girl, May Tanner, whose father owned a second-hand furniture shop.

Of their wedding, the *Cork County Eagle and Munster Advertiser* reported in November 1911, 'The bride and groom are very well known in Dunmanway district, Miss May Tanner being extremely popular. Since the bridegroom's sojourn in the district he has become a great favourite and endeared himself to all. As owner of the Medical Hall he has made a host of friends, being very obliging, with a kind and pleasant word for everyone. We wish the happy pair many years of conjugal happiness.'

That was not to be. A year after giving birth to a son, Walter, in 1913, May died at twenty-eight of a miscarriage. Her monument in the Dunmanway churchyard is of astonishing taste and beauty, a sophisticated jewel in this Irish country town. It must have cost David everything he had. On it is the pathetic inscription,

We cannot, Lord, your purpose see,
But all is well that's done by thee.

David was a single father, a businessman, a member of the Parish Council, and also a Mason. The Masonic lodge of Bandon had connections – but extremely loose ones - with the Orange Lodges of the North. Protestantism in the south of Ireland was, and still is, rather middle-class and British, and has little relationship to the big drums, bowler hats and sashes of Ulster.

Three years later David married again, and his second wife, my grandmother, was an outstanding character of great strength, talent and practical humanity.

Alice Anderson, a year older than David, was a twin. She and her sister, Kathleen, were assistants in the grocery shop. Their father Samuel, a gamekeeper, was working away from home. He left his wife, Mary Letitia, to run a lodging house and tea rooms in Main Street, opposite the Anglican church. Alice's two schoolboy brothers, Edward and Cecil, were Irish speakers. The lodgers were two Scottish commercial travellers who 'professed no religion', and a Jewish dealer in cutlery and jewellery, who had been born in Russian Poland. It pleases me that there was a Jewish influence in my grandmother's upbringing.

Mary Letitia Anderson, Alice's mother, had been born into the mainstream Protestant Ascendancy. Her father, Richard Becher Orpen, had ended up as the factor on the estate - Sillahertane - that he had once owned. Like many of the Irish gentry, his money had been lost during the Great Famine, when death and emigration had destroyed so many estates. All his life he described himself as a 'gentleman'.

The first Richard Orpen had been brought to Kerry from Somerset in the 1660s by his mentor, the great paternalist landlord and father of economics, Sir William Petty. He became his agent. A more glamorous (if distant) ancestor, Sanchet D'Abrichecourt, was a founder Knight of the Order of the Garter.

Mary Letitia's cousins included the painter Sir William Orpen, and Charlotte Payne-Townshend, the wife of George Bernard Shaw. She attended the school that her grandfather had built for the children of the poor, and it educated her well. Her obituary, which remarked that she came from a 'fine old family', also declared her to be 'highly educated, charitable, broad-minded, of refined and cultured tastes'. She wrote poetry with the vocabulary of *The English Hymnal*, but with an emotional force and deep power that moves me very much. Most of her poems deal with death, a subject about which she knew, as two of her ten children had died in infancy. They were lost in girlhood to the tuberculosis so prevalent in Ireland, and one son (my great-uncle Arthur, whose photograph I have by my bed) was to be killed in Flanders in 1918.

A year after David and Alice married, twins were born - Evelyn and Reginald - in a birth that was obviously precarious, as they were baptised at home on the same day. Then three years later, in May 1920, was born a daughter, Irene Violet. She gave birth, in time, to me.

Alice was a musician who, had she received proper training, would have been of professional standard. In church she played the organ and was the choir mistress.

Their quiet and ordered provincial life was lived against a background of great and terrible events. During the War of Independence of 1919-1921, West Cork was one of the most violent parts of Ireland and the scene of many of the conflict's major actions. Dunmanway was the home of K Company of the Auxiliaries - the dreaded Black and Tans - whose barracks were the old Dunmanway Workhouse. This regiment was the real scum of the British army. Most of the soldiers were veterans of the Great War. Some were seriously shell-shocked working-class lads from industrial cities, who had no idea why they were in Ireland or what the fight was about. They had been told that the Irish were a bunch of cunning, murderous savages, whom they must kill before they were killed. The regiment was appallingly badly commanded, and its position in the British army was so low that its soldiers didn't even have proper uniforms; hence the policemen's jackets and regulation brown trousers that gave them their nickname.

What happened in Ireland in the first quarter of the twentieth century was truly terrible, and - it has to be said - was caused entirely by three centuries of English tyranny over the disempowered and disenfranchised Roman Catholic majority.

In politics, David was not a Unionist or a Loyalist but a Free-Stater. He believed that Ireland should be self-governing but linked to the British crown, and that it should have Dominion status like Canada. But to the Republicans, the Free-Staters were as pernicious as any Unionist, perhaps even more so: the enemy who were nearly friends.

David also wanted to move himself into the professional class. He wanted the best for himself, his family and for Ireland.

In 1921 the Peace Treaty had been signed, and Michael Collins's provisional government was in place. Ireland was indeed now a free state. But the hotch-potch of delegates who made up the *Dáil* were split on the validity of the Treaty. Consequently, it was put to a vote that the government won. The Republicans, who wanted complete disestablishment, were angry and dissatisfied.

By 1922, the Royal Irish Constabulary had been disbanded and, until the Garda were formed six months later, Ireland was without a police force - except for the I.R.A. The I.R.A. was directing traffic in Cork, Limerick, and Dublin!

Also in 1922, K Company was withdrawn from its Dunmanway headquarters, and the local I.R.A. moved in to see what they could find. They claimed that they had discovered documents listing local Protestant 'friends' of the British army, who were possibly informers. At the top of the list, they claimed, were three names, and one of them was David Gray's. These documents have never been found or seen, and historians of different persuasions have argued over their existence.

One Republican historian claimed that an old lady had told her that, as a ten-year-old girl, she was warned against chatting with David 'in spite of his kindness'. 'He sought information from children in their innocence.' What information? 'Who is staying in your house? Who are your Da's friends?'

However, David had undeniably met the officers in church, provided them with medical supplies, and, with Alice, had entertained and been entertained by them. For a young man like David, dining with a major or a captain had real social distinction.

In April 1922, the I.R.A high command who, for the most, consisted of law-abiding patriots (and surprisingly a Church of Ireland clergyman), went to Dublin for a conference, leaving the boys on the ground in charge. These boys decided that there was unfinished business in West Cork.

On April 26, at two o'clock in the morning, a group of them arrived at the house of a local farmer, a widower and former magistrate called Thomas Hornibrook. They tried to commandeer his car. Mr. Hornibrook's son Samuel and son-in-law Herbert Woods (a former captain in the British army) were at home. The car had been disabled against such an eventuality. The gang's leader, Michael O'Neill, demanded that the missing part be restored. When this was refused, the I.R.A. group climbed in through a window. O'Neill was shot fatally by Herbert Woods. The I.R.A. boys carried him to a priest, who could only pronounce him dead.

They then, supplemented by reinforcements, returned to the house and surrounded it with about a hundred men. A shoot-out ensued. When the Hornibrooks ran out of ammunition, they surrendered. Herbert Woods was tried by a kangaroo court, found guilty, and shot, probably after being tortured.

The Hornibrooks, father and son, were driven to a remote spot and made to kneel. They were then shot in the back of their heads. Their bodies were never found.

Next the group turned its attention to nearby Dunmanway and the three men apparently named in the Workhouse document. First to be shot outside his house was Francis Fitzmaurice, a solicitor. Then they went to Sackville Street and forced an elderly retired draper, James Buttimer, to come downstairs to his front door. 'Boys, boys, you wouldn't want to harm an old man,' he pleaded. They did. He was shot in the head, his brains spattering his wife, who was standing beside him.

Next door lived the Grays. It was three o'clock in the morning.

The group shouted for David to come downstairs. He, Alice, and the children were upstairs.

He came downstairs and stood in the doorway. 'Take that, you Free-Stater,' said the gunman, and shot him in the chest. He fell half in, half out of the house. Alice stayed upstairs for a long while, uncertain if the men had gone. When she came downstairs, she saw that David was dead. Did the children hear their father murdered? Walter was nine, the twins five, and Irene not quite two.

I stood in that doorway eighty years later, taking part in an R.T.E. documentary. I was in a detached, professional, talking head frame of mind, when I suddenly felt absolute cold horror and paralysing fear. I was picking up the traces of my grandfather's terror from eighty years before. I had vaguely imagined David as being a strong and very masculine man, but I knew with a certainty then that then he had felt such fear as I have since felt - but over far lesser things. It was at that moment that I loved him.

Then the I.R.A. foot soldiers went berserk. Eight more Protestants in the district were killed the next day. Two of them were sixteen years old.

The killings were universally condemned: by Michael Collins and Eamon de Valera in Dublin, by the press in London and New York, and tacitly by the senior I.R.A., who returned to Cork with the draconian edict that if there were any further killings, the murderers would be shot themselves. The extraordinary result of this edict was that Protestant houses were guarded by I.R.A. soldiers. Nonetheless, the Dunmanway killers were never caught - nor, it is believed, was much effort made to catch them.

The aftermath of Dunmanway was a Protestant diaspora. Nearly a hundred families left, for the

North, for London, or for Canada, some with only the clothes they stood up in and the possessions they could carry.

Other Protestants fled, but Alice and her family remained in Dunmanway until after her mother's death in 1926, when they moved north to Rockcorry in Monaghan. This was near to where both her father's and husband's families had originated from. She was far luckier than most. The family were given an apartment in a beautiful Georgian almshouse opposite the church, where she became the organist. Her children sang in the choir.

The Masons stepped in, and gave the children an education that they probably would not have received had their father lived. Indeed, the boys, destined for the church, were given the best that Ireland could offer: school at Portora Royal, then University at Trinity College Dublin. Walter became Rector of Newbliss and Kileevan (where he was known as a great preacher and fund-raiser), and then a chaplain in the R.A.F. In understandable reaction to his father's murder, he became a staunch Orangeman and opponent of the I.R.A. He died of a heart attack at the age of thirty-nine, leaving a widow and a three-year old son, Stephen. Reginald, a divinity student at Trinity, joined the R.A.F. during the war and stayed on. His speciality was dealing with bereaved families. Later, he married an English girl and settled in Hampshire with his wife and son, David. Alice died in 1943 of cancer and diabetes, at the age of sixty.

Irene won a scholarship to the Collegiate School, Celbridge, the best girl's school in Ireland, and then trained as a nurse. Evelyn, who was briefly a woman soldier, became the companion and adopted daughter of Rockcorry's most prominent resident.

Lady Edith Windham-Dawson was the only daughter of the second Earl of Dartrey. She was a widow and lived in great splendour at the heart of eleven thousand acres in a neo-Elizabethan house, Dawson's Grove. This she eventually abandoned for a smaller one. Lady Edith's first husband had been the Honourable Charles Douglas-Pennant, whose family owned the Penrhyn quarries on the other side of Elidir Mountain to the Dinorwic quarries. Their house, Penrhyn Castle, was half an hour's drive from Vaynol. Lady Edith and my grandmother Juliet were exact contemporaries. She spent the First World War at Penrhyn and London, just as Juliet spent it at Vaynol and London, and both their husbands were killed in action. The two *must* have known each other. Michael *must* have met Lady Edith as a boy.

Evelyn dressed in man's clothes and worked in the garden. The two ladies rescued and looked after animals, many of whose graves are to be still found on the estate. Lady Edith kept an eye on her companion's family and assisted them financially, getting Stephen his first leg-up in the world of banking, which was to be his career. But where her help was perhaps most required was in Irene's case.

Irene, who loved drama and poetry, trained as a social worker. She was pretty and independent, five-foot-seven tall with red-brown hair. According to her nephew Stephen, she was friendly, open and sociable. She drove a baby Austin, drank gin and tonics, and smoked Passing Cloud cigarettes.

She worked first in Dublin. There she met an academic, probably of native Irish and French-Jewish descent. She became pregnant.

Lady Edith stepped in. Irene went to London to lodge with a clergyman of the Church of Ireland called the Reverend Thomas Horan, who was then a Canon of Southwark Cathedral. Her son was born at St James's Hospital, Battersea. She called him Jonathan, after Swift, for whom she had lifelong admiration. She also thought the gloomy Dean's edge of temperament and skill as a satirist would be of use to me. She then returned to Ireland, leaving me with the Horans. Irene Carisbrooke's efforts found me, and my new mother's sister, Liz von Hofmannsthal, came to check that I had two arms, two legs, and a head. I had, and I was just ten weeks old when I was handed over to that family, who, I have never doubted, for good or ill, became entirely my own.

Irene returned to Dublin and became a social therapist (the first they had ever had) at St. Patrick's Hospital, the lunatic asylum famously founded by Swift:

He gave the little wealth he had,
To build a house for fools and mad;

And shew'd by one satiric touch,
No nation wanted it so much.

Irene introduced the new therapy of 'role-play' to Ireland. She was a great champion of this technique, often giving workshops and demonstrations. She also wrote a play, *Silhouette*, about Oliver Goldsmith, from whose brother she believed she was descended. This play was twice performed by patients.

Irene Gray died suddenly of a brain haemorrhage in December 1962, when she was forty-two years old and I was just thirteen. Much loved, she was given a great funeral at St. Patrick's Cathedral.

Lady Edith died in 1974, after adopting Evelyn as her daughter. In spite of this, Lady Edith's relations and executor turfed her out of the house destitute, without a penny and without a memento. Until 1980, adopted children had no right to parents' estates. She found refuge with two sisters who were church friends of hers, and there she lived until her death twelve years later, subsisting on Irene's small pension from St. Patrick's Hospital. She was buried as 'Evelyn Dawson' in the Dawson family plot.

Stephen Gray is now my friend, as is Reggie's son David, both respectable bachelors who worked in banking: Stephen in Dublin, David in Hampshire.

I, the son of an academic and a social worker, am now an academic (and, for my later career, at a Roman Catholic University too). I have no immediate family, and am thus interested in my students' lives. So I suppose I am a sort of social worker too.

Dunmanway was the town where Caroline and her lesbian friends had lunch that day in 1949, when, heavily pregnant, and only a few months after her marriage, she wanted a holiday away from Michael. They stayed with Rachel Leigh-White, who through the Bechers was a distant biological cousin of mine!

There was quite a lot of publicity in fashionable magazines about my adoption when I was a child. Did any copies of *The Sunday Pictorial* or *The Tatler* ever find their way to Dawson's Grove? Did Lady Edith stay in touch with her first husband's family? Did the Grays know about me?

After Michael Duff died in 1980, I asked for and was given my original birth certificate and adoption papers, such as there were. Only twenty years later did I try to find out more. Caroline knew that Irene's brother was a clergyman, and Crockford's Clerical Directory of 1949 provided me with two Grays in Ireland, one of them Walter. The widow of his successor as Rector of Newbliss started me on the search that led first to my second cousin Maureen, who lives in Canada. ('Now isn't that wonderful!' she said when I told her that she was the first blood relative I had ever spoken to.) Then it led to Stephen, my first cousin in Dublin. When he and I first met at Dublin airport, it was strange to see my own eyes looking back at me.

I think of Charley and David as my grandfathers (and I bet the English Marquess and Irish pharmacist would have liked and respected each other). I think of Juliet and Alice as my grandmothers. I think of Louisa and David as my cousins.

But for all the sympathy I have for Irene and her lecturer, I think of Michael and Caroline as my parents.

FIN

MY FAMILY OF ORIGIN

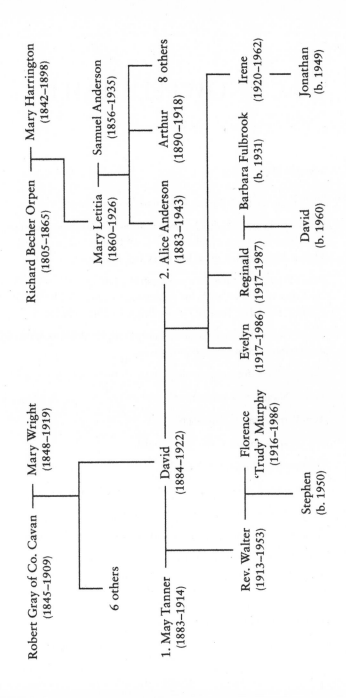

ACKNOWLEDGEMENTS

I would like to thank:

My cousin Victoria Taylor, who made it all possible.

The Cecil Beaton Studio Archive at Sotheby's, for permission to reproduce five photographs by Sir Cecil Beaton, and its curator, Joanna Ling, for her great kindness and assistance.

Peters Fraser & Dunlop (www.petersfraserdunlop.com) on behalf of the Estate of Hilaire Belloc for permission to reprint 'FAREWELL TO JULIET' from *The Verse of Hilaire Belloc* by Hilaire Belloc.

Hugo Vickers for permission to quote from Cecil Beaton's diaries, and for his encouragement and advice.

Gareth Dorey, for keeping me going.

Louise Naudé, first-rate editor.

Tom Perrin, star of publishers.

Jean Peyton, indefatigable genealogist.

Christopher Phipps, for the index.

Kevin Trainor, who read an earlier draft and was sensible.

Elizabeth Vickers, for the photographic reproductions.

George Vickers, for design work and further photographic assistance.

Every effort has been made to obtain permissions for the copyright materials, both illustrative and quoted. If there have been any omissions in this respect, the publishers and author offer their sincere regrets and will be pleased to ensure that an appropriate acknowledgement will appear in any future edition.

INDEX

Charles Duff was born in 1949. His first book, *The Lost Summer*, was a history of the West End in the 1940s and 1950s. He is also an actor, a lecturer in Shakespeare and theatre history, and a contributor to the national press on arts-related subjects.

He has lived between Los Angeles, London, Paris and Tangier and he is now a Brother of the London Charterhouse.